Women's Lives in Biblical Times

Women's Lives in Biblical Times

Jennie R. Ebeling

t&t clark

Published by T&T International
A Continuum Imprint

The Tower Building	80 Maiden Lane
11 York Road	Suite 704
London SE1 7NX	New York NY 10038

www.continuumbooks.com

First published 2010
Reprinted 2011

Jennie R. Ebeling has asserted her right under the Copyright, Designs and Patents Act, 1988, to be identified as the Author of this work.

British Library Cataloguing-in-Publication Data
A catalogue record for this book is available from the British Library

ISBN: 978-0-567-39830-7 (Hardback)
    978-0-567-19644-6 (Paperback)

Typeset by Pindar NZ, Auckland, New Zealand
Printed and bound in the United States of America

Contents

Contents

Preface

This book was conceived in the fiction section of my local Barnes and Noble. As I strolled through the aisles, reading titles, I was surprised to see a number of recent works of historical fiction that focused on female biblical characters, much like Anita Diamant's successful novel *The Red Tent* (St. Martin's Press, 1997). After collecting a stack of these books and skimming through them, I was frustrated by the authors' lack of attempt to present a reasonable reconstruction of women's lives in ancient Israel, and I felt a bit sorry for the biblical women — among them Sarah, Rebekah, Miriam and Deborah — whose imagined lives were so full of romanticized drama. Then and there I began to sketch an outline of this book that integrated a narrative account of one woman's life in ancient Israel into an academic discussion of what we really know about the lives of biblical women based on recent research in biblical studies, archaeology, iconography and ethnography. Although I knew I would not create a story as dramatic — and thus as potentially best-selling — as those published by the fiction writers, I felt that I could convey the reality of women's everyday experiences in ancient Israel, which is infinitely more interesting (to me, anyway).

However, I was aware that those with a similar perspective to mine — the archaeologists and biblical scholars with years of experience in their fields — had not done an adequate job of translating what we know of women's lives in ancient Israel to the student and lay reader. Several recent books on daily life in ancient Israel meant to be accessible to a broad audience, for example, did not systematically consider women's lives, and the authors — several of them archaeologists — still looked to the Hebrew Bible (Old Testament) as a primary source or the only source of information. This approach results in an incomplete and inaccurate portrayal of Israelite women that allows for an elitist and androcentric view of life in ancient Israel to persist. Other recent works on women in ancient Israel, which are written primarily by biblical scholars, do not always take the vast non-textual sources into consideration and tend to focus on women's religious lives. Although I discuss women's religious experiences in this book, they are not my primary focus; instead, I examine the complexity of women's everyday experiences using a variety of sources of information and not confining myself to the incomplete biblical descriptions.

My interest in women in ancient Israel stems from my expertise in food preparation technology, specifically the analysis of the ground stone tools used to process grain and other foodstuffs for consumption in antiquity. In addition to participating in archaeological excavations in Israel, I have served as a ground stone artifact specialist for over a dozen excavation and publication projects in Israel for more than a decade. Cross-culturally, women are most closely associated with ground stone tools in traditional societies, and these seemingly mundane tools found in large quantities in Bronze and Iron Age sites in Israel can reveal much about the lives of the women who used them for up to several hours per day. My interest in "women's work" in the sphere of cooking led me to further investigate women's involvement in other ancient technologies and their resulting economic contributions to the Israelite household. In this book, I discuss women's control of such diverse crafts and technologies as pottery production, spinning, weaving, basketry and hide working, along with women's essential contributions in the realms of midwifery, birth, breastfeeding, childrearing and household ritual, and their participation in supposedly male activities like harvesting and processing grain, grapes, olives and other crops. These and many other activities occupied the daily lives of women living in the central highland villages of early Israel during the Iron Age I (c. 1200–1000 BCE).

This book was written while teaching for the Department of Archaeology and Art History at the University of Evansville in the 2007–8 academic year and during a sabbatical semester spent in Evansville in fall 2008. I thank the students enrolled in my "Daily Life in Biblical Times" class in spring 2008 for their feedback on a draft of one chapter and their perspectives on the presentation of daily life in ancient Israel in recent popular and academic publications. Thanks go to several colleagues who also read drafts, and to Mollie Erickson, who not only drew the map and reinterpreted the images used in this book from the originals but also read and took notes on a number of the recent novels about biblical women, a large and sometimes frustrating task for which I am grateful. The unparalleled contributions of Carol Meyers to the study of Israelite women have provided much inspiration for my own recent research, and I thank her for her enthusiasm for this project. I also thank Beth Alpert Nakhai for her support, advice and friendship over the years and Bill Dever for championing me since my first semester as a graduate student at the University of Arizona. Thanks also go to Burke Gerstenschlager and Dominic Mattos for working with me on this project, and offering advice and enthusiasm during the process. This book is dedicated to my parents, Ginny Ebeling and Bill Ebeling, my brother Todd and sister Ashly, as well as the members of my *bet 'em* (or *bet 'ab*, depending on the day): Menachem, Lilah and Aviva Rogel.

Abbreviations

ABD	*Anchor Bible Dictionary*, ed. D.N. Freedman. 6 vols. New York: Doubleday, 1992.
AEMT	*Ancient Egyptian Materials and Technologies*, eds. P.T. Nicholson and I. Shaw. Cambridge: Cambridge University Press, 2000.
BA	*Biblical Archaeologist*
BASOR	*Bulletin of the American Schools of Oriental Research*
CANE	*Civilizations of the Ancient Near East*, ed. J.M. Sasson. 4 vols. New York: Charles Scribner's Sons, 1995.
IEJ	*Israel Exploration Journal*
JBL	*Journal of Biblical Literature*
JNES	*Journal of Near Eastern Studies*
JPOS	*Journal of the Palestinian Oriental Society*
NEA	*Near Eastern Archaeology*
NEAEHL	*New Encyclopedia of Archaeological Excavations in the Holy Land*, ed. E. Stern. 4 vols. New York: Simon and Schuster, 1993.
OEANE	*Oxford Encyclopedia of Archaeology in the Near East*, ed. E.M. Meyers. 5 vols. New York: Oxford University Press, 1997.
VT	*Vetus Testamentum*
WA	*World Archaeology*
WIS	*Women in Scripture: A Dictionary of Named and Unnamed Women in the Hebrew Bible, the Apocryphal/Deuterocanonical Books, and the New Testament*, eds. C.L. Meyers, T. Craven and R.S. Kraemer. Boston: Houghton Mifflin, 2000.

List of Figures

Introduction

This book presents a reconstruction of the life of a fictional woman named Orah — which is Hebrew for "light" — in a small village in the central highlands of Iron Age I Israel (c. 1200–1000 BCE). Its seven chapters chronicle her life "from cradle to grave," focusing on the events, customs, crafts and technologies, and other activities in which Israelite women would have participated on a daily basis according to the agricultural calendar by which they lived. Each chapter opens with a brief fictional narrative — "Orah's Story" — about Orah at different ages, and the rest of the chapter consists of a scholarly discussion of the evidence for the events and activities described in the narrative using archaeology, the Hebrew Bible (Old Testament) and other ancient Near Eastern and Egyptian texts, iconography and ethnography from the modern Middle East. This book is thus a scholarly work about the everyday lives of women in ancient Israel, but also a uniquely accessible and engaging reconstruction for anyone interested in women's lives in biblical times.

Existing Studies of Women in Iron Age/Biblical Israel

I have written this book in response to three recent types of publications concerning women's lives in the period of the Hebrew Bible: academic works about biblical women written primarily by scholars of the Bible; academic works about daily life in ancient Israel written by Syro-Palestinian (or "biblical") archaeologists and biblical scholars; and fictional accounts of the lives of specific female biblical characters written by novelists with little to no academic background in the history, culture and religion of ancient Israel.

Academic Works about Biblical Women

The numerous scholarly publications about the lives of biblical women and women in ancient Israel, many of which are currently used in undergraduate courses, are written primarily by biblical scholars and thus rely on the

Hebrew Bible as the main — or only — source of evidence.[1] Although the Hebrew Bible is an important a source when reconstructing certain aspects of women's lives in ancient Israel, it provides little to no information about many of the daily-life activities that occupied the women and girls who lived in the early Israelite villages and female lifecycle events (see further below). Indeed, any study that does not utilize the information from extra-biblical sources — such as other texts from the ancient Near East and Egypt, archaeological remains, iconographic representations and ethnographic accounts — can only provide a partial account of what everyday life may have been like for a typical Israelite woman.[2]

Since one of the main foci of the biblical writers was the relationship between the ancient Israelites and their national god, Yahweh, we can assume that a number of biblical stories about or concerning women have a theological intent. As a result, perhaps, biblical scholars have shown great interest in reconstructing women's religious lives, including women's partici-pation in public and private cultic activities and events.[3] Although I describe women's religious experiences both in the household context and in the public realm throughout this book, this is not my primary focus; instead, I reconstruct the reality of women's everyday experiences and mainly describe religious practices as they relate to female lifecycle events, like coming of age (Chapter 3), childbirth (Chapter 5), weaning (Chapter 6) and death (Chapter 7). Integrating women's religious activities into my discussion of more "mundane" everyday activities also serves to illustrate how religious belief and practice may have permeated daily life in ancient Israel.[4]

Academic Works about Daily Life in Iron Age/Biblical Israel

In addition to these scholarly works on biblical women, several books on life in biblical times written by biblical scholars and archaeologists working at sites in Israel have recently appeared. The two most important works are Oded Borowski's *Daily Life in Biblical Times* (2003) and Philip J. King and Lawrence E. Stager's *Life in Biblical Israel* (2001), and both are accessible vol-umes that endeavor to reconstruct aspects of daily life in ancient Israel using a variety of sources. However, neither work systematically considers gender issues or topics relevant to the study of Israelite women, such as women's contributions to the household economy (Nakhai 2005). Although both use archaeological, ethnographic and extra-biblical sources of information throughout, the authors have a tendency to privilege the Hebrew Bible as a source of information about women's lives, which is problematic for a number of reasons (below). Interestingly, both Borowski and King and Stager include fictional sketches of daily life in ancient Israel in their books — King and Stager include a brief reconstruction of a day in the life in Micah's house (inspired by Judges 17–18) and Borowski devotes his last chapter to a "day-in-the-life" story set in the Iron Age — but they do not focus on women's activities specifically.[5]

Fictional Accounts of Biblical Women

Outside of the realm of scholarly works on biblical women and daily life in ancient Israel are a number of recent novels about the lives of female biblical characters.[6] This trend, which appears to have begun with Anita Diamant's *The Red Tent* (1997), shows that there is great public interest in dramatized accounts of biblical women's lives (Klein 2007). The adoption of works like *The Red Tent*, which is a fictional account of the life of Dinah (Gen. 34. 24–31), by university instructors teaching introductory courses on the Old Testament/Hebrew Bible, women in the Bible and the like into their curricula demonstrates that such narratives are useful tools for engaging students in the subject of biblical women. However, these books are not written by biblical scholars or other specialists in ancient Israelite culture, and much of the information presented in the stories is idiosyncratic if not completely inaccurate. Certainly these novels are not intended to be scholarly discussions of biblical women's lives, but I am afraid that many readers believe that these stories contain accurate representations of the past.

Works from all three of these categories can be useful in reconstructing women's lives in biblical times,[7] and I used many publications from the first two categories in researching this book and suggest them for further reading. However, none of these sources provide an up-to-date, comprehensive discussion of what we know about women in ancient Israel using all available sources of evidence.

How This Book is Different

This book is similar to those in the first two categories in that it focuses specifically on women and everyday life activities in ancient Israel, but differs from them in its goal of creating a comprehensive reconstruction of one hypothetical woman's life experiences using archaeology as a primary source. In addition, this book uses fictional narrative like the works in the third category to engage student and lay readers and "bring the past to life," but is distinctive because it is written by a specialist in ancient Israelite history, culture and religion and includes scholarly discussions of the information presented in the fictional passages. This book thus serves as a supplement to traditional textbooks employed in introductory-level courses on the Old Testament/Hebrew Bible that include relatively little information about women's lives, and it can also stand alone as an accessible discussion of women in ancient Israel for use in women's studies courses or courses on the history of ancient Israel. It is unique in that both the narrative and the scholarly discussion focus on the major events in a woman's life from birth to death with an emphasis on the relationship between daily life activities and the agricultural calendar, and because each chapter is set in a different season, starting with the spring barley harvest and ending during the winter sowing season.

The greatest contribution of this book is its use of a wide range of sources of evidence to reconstruct women's activities and lifecycle events in the Iron Age. Used in tandem with the textual and iconographic sources from ancient Israel and neighboring lands, as well as ethnographic analogies from Palestine and neighboring countries in the nineteenth and twentieth centuries, archaeology is a particularly important resource for reconstructing women's activities and experiences in ancient Israel. Carol Meyers has shown this best in her recent studies of women's control of bread baking in the household context (Meyers 2002a, 2003a, 2007) and activities related to textile production, including spinning and weaving (Meyers 2003a); in these studies, she looks to ethnography, ethnohistory and iconography to help determine the gendered — specifically, female-gendered — use of artifacts (Meyers 2002a, 20). Archaeology provides unique and often abundant sources of information on female crafts and technologies like cooking and producing textiles, but also brewing beer, producing pottery, working hides, weaving baskets and more. The biblical text is largely silent on women's contributions to these important everyday activities in the ancient Israelite villages.

The brief narrative account presented at the beginning of each chapter is primarily intended to stimulate interest in the scholarly discussion that follows. Given the explosion of recent fictional accounts of biblical women's lives and the successful use of some of these works in academic courses, it seems useful to integrate a story into an academic discussion of women's lives that is intended primarily for a student and lay audience. Although I do not claim that every detail in the narrative is confirmed by archaeology and other sources, I use a variety of evidence to create as accurate a picture of life in ancient Israel as possible and I provide rationale for the descriptions in the narrative throughout the book. The main character in the story, Orah, is not an individual known to us from the Hebrew Bible; instead, she represents what I imagine to have been a typical woman living in a small village in the central highlands of early Israel during the period of the Judges (see further below). Some of the events in her life are inspired by biblical passages — such as Chapter 6, elements of which are based on the story of Hannah as it appears in 1 Samuel — but other sources provide many of the details in the stories as well. The reader is encouraged to consult the sources listed in the "For Further Reading" sections at the end of each chapter as well as the other bibliographic sources for more information. And, of course, the reader should also see the relevant passages from the New Revised Standard Version of the Hebrew Bible that I cite throughout.[8]

The chapters of the book follow the chapters in Orah's life from her birth to her death so that women's contributions and activities at various ages can be explored. One of the most important, I feel, is Chapter 2, which is set when Orah is eight years old; in this chapter, we discover how she is taught to perform three of the essential tasks required of women living in ancient Israelite villages — producing food and drink, pottery and textiles — at an early age. Indeed, much of a girl's early education consisted of "instruction" in these crafts and activities to prepare her for her future roles as wife and mother, and her "practice" serves to assist her mother and other female family members with these time-consuming household tasks. Archaeological remains and other sources offer important clues for reconstructing these crucial daily activities in the lives of Israelite women and girls. Multiple sources also inform my discussion of the lifecycle events in which Orah participates at various ages, including menstruation (Chapter 3), marriage (Chapter 4) and childbirth (Chapter 5), as well as the events that surrounded her final, fatal illness and death (Chapter 7).

Setting each chapter in a specific agricultural season primarily serves to emphasize the importance of the agricultural calendar in the lives of the Israelite villagers, a fact that is hinted at in the Gezer Calendar, which is one of the earliest known Hebrew inscriptions (Chapter 1). Orah's life begins at a symbolic point of "rebirth" in the agricultural year — during the spring barley harvest and just after the first harvest festival of the year — and ends during the rainy winter season, when the villagers are occupied with sowing grain to be harvested the following spring. Setting each chapter in a different time of year allows me to focus on how women's lives were affected by each agricultural season, and examine women's roles in activities like laboring in the fields and agricultural terraces during the harvest seasons, preserving agricultural products at home for year-round use, participating in seasonal festivals and more. Focusing on specific agricultural seasons has also allowed me to integrate the celebration of the three major festivals in the religious calendar known from the Hebrew Bible, *massot/pessah*, *shevuot* and *'asip/sukkot*, all of which had agricultural origins. Since women participated in these festivals along with men (Chapter 1), they would have been very important events in women's lives at prescribed times each year.

The Sources

I will now briefly discuss the sources that informed my reconstruction of the events in Orah's life. These include archaeology, the Hebrew Bible and other ancient Near Eastern and Egyptian texts, iconography and ethnography.

Archaeology

Using archaeological remains to reconstruct women's lives in the ancient Near East generally and in Syria-Palestine[9] specifically is a relatively recent endeavor. There are a number of reasons why this is the case. A central reason relates to the methodology of the (mostly male) archaeologists working in the region since the nineteenth century who used the Hebrew Bible to set the agendas for their excavations. Since the biblical writers were primarily concerned with the world of the urban male elite, male archaeologists, with their primarily text-driven interests, focused their attention on the identification and excavation of monumental architecture like the palaces, temples and fortification systems described in the Bible instead of the houses and other domestic structures and areas built and used by the common people. As a result, there exists a gap in our knowledge of the lives of most of the Israelite population, especially women and men living in villages and other non-urban settings.

Attempts to identify the archaeological correlates of the large-scale political and social processes described in the Hebrew Bible have thus led to the general neglect of the smaller-scale issues associated with the household. The long-held misconception that public life is always more masculine or closely associated with males than private life, which is more closely associated with women, and that the masculine realm is somehow more important than the feminine realm, has contributed to this problem. Although recent interest in "household archaeology" and the excavation of villages and farmsteads has led to more knowledge of the peasant peoples who made up the majority of the Iron Age population in Israel, little attention has been paid to the gendered activities that were carried out in domestic settings (Meyers 2003b, 186–87). Even though households are now considered legitimate contexts for archaeological investigations, few researchers to date have systematically focused on identifying "women's spaces" in Iron Age houses.

Another reason why archaeology has neglected the study of women concerns the continuing focus of Syro-Palestinian archaeologists on diachronic changes, or changes through time. Archaeologists have long emphasized stratigraphic excavation and artifact typologies — especially ceramic typologies (Chapter 2) — and not the analysis of artifact assemblages from a specific archaeological context. This is readily apparent in the format of most excavation reports, which include chapters written by different material culture specialists in pottery, metals, stone tools etc., that are separate from the stratigraphic discussion and conclusions/syntheses. This stymies attempts to identify women's spaces and activities within a house, for example, because the researcher must examine all of the published information in the excavation report and perhaps elsewhere to reconstruct the contents of, say, a single room; this can be a painstaking, and sometimes impossible, exercise that few researchers have attempted (Meyers 2003b, 187–90).

Perhaps not surprisingly, female scholars have been and continue to be most interested in gender issues, and the continuing disparity between male and female academics in salary, publication and grant opportunities, and domestic responsibilities have negatively impacted their study of Israelite women (Nakhai 2007, 513–14). This is also relevant with regard to the study of biblical women by female biblical scholars (below).

Archaeology has great potential to inform on women's lives, however, and with a shift in methodology toward total recovery of materials and new publication strategies (see further Meyers 2003b) we can learn much about the everyday life activities of both females and males in household settings in particular. As household archaeology develops, we are certain to learn more about the domestic economy, household crafts and technologies, and related issues and activities in the early Iron Age. Since women are believed to have been more closely associated with certain daily domestic activities like cooking and producing textiles than men during the Iron Age — although women's labor was also needed in the fields and terraces surrounding the ancient villages, as we shall see — we should expect to find the archaeological remains of women's activities in these structures. Engendering ancient activities and activity areas is difficult, and requires the use of analogies derived from multiple sources, but strides made by archaeologists working in other parts of the world demonstrate how fruitful an endeavor this can be (cf. Meyers 2003b).

In some cases, archaeological remains from neighboring lands like Egypt, where the arid environment has allowed for the preservation of ancient organic remains, provide much useful information for female activities like textile production, basket weaving, and hide working that do not leave clear traces in the archaeological record of Syria-Palestine, which has a more variable climate. I look to the archaeological evidence from the region under discussion whenever possible in this study, although I use the relevant remains from ancient Egypt, the Mediterranean world and other parts of the ancient Near East as well.

Hebrew Bible and Other Ancient Near Eastern and Egyptian Texts

Another source for reconstructing the lives of women in ancient Israel is, of course, the Hebrew Bible. It is only in recent decades, however, that biblical scholars and archaeologists have looked to the biblical text for information about Israelite women. The reasons why Israelite women have been over-looked — or completely ignored, one could argue, until relatively recently — are numerous, but a central problem is that, in the past, most biblical scholars were men and their interests did not often include the everyday lives of women living in the Iron Age. Even today, when there are more women in the field of biblical studies and more female archaeologists working in the region than ever before, the study of Israelite women lags behind the study of women in other ancient cultures (Nakhai 2007, 513).

Recent contributions by feminist biblical scholars and others, however, clearly demonstrate that scripture provides many avenues for research into biblical women, including historically oriented analyses (as opposed to literary-critical methodologies) that ask "what we can ascertain from Hebrew Bible texts regarding the actual lives and experiences of ancient Israelite women" (Ackerman 2003, 172). Certainly no serious scholar of ancient Israel would discuss Israelite women without using the biblical text as a source, but we must keep in mind the reasons why the Hebrew Bible is problematic for investigating the daily life activities of women living in ancient Israel.

A fundamental problem is that the Hebrew Bible is male-oriented in authorship, subject matter and perspectives. The androcentric (male-centered) nature of the Hebrew Bible is made clear in a count of personal names that appear in the text: of 1,426 names, 111 are women's names, which is 9 percent of the total (Meyers 1998, 251–52). The men who composed these texts were primarily concerned with the world of the urban male elite — kings, priests, prophets and others — and the relationship between the people of Israel and their national god, Yahweh. Generally speaking, these male authors did not consider the common people — those peasants who comprised the majority of the population of Israel and Judah — important enough to describe in detail. The biblical writers certainly did not set out to write a manual of daily life in ancient Israel, and the text "does not provide accurate, systematic, or complete records of the daily lives of most people, male as well as female" (Meyers 2002a, 15). The extra-biblical textual sources from ancient Israel unearthed in archaeological excavations and explorations also show no indication of female authorship, and we thus lack any textual witness to the lives and experiences of Israelite women in their own words (Ackerman 2003, 174).

The biblical writers did describe some exceptional female characters that played important roles in shaping Israel's history and traditions, from the named matriarchs in Genesis and the Judge Deborah in Israel's early history, to the queens and prophetesses of the monarchic era. But these female characters are precisely that — exceptional — and probably do not reflect the reality of most women in ancient Israel, especially those living in the villages of the central highlands. The biblical text provides bits of information that inform on women's lives — including marriage customs, childbirth rituals, midwifery, childrearing practices, religious activities and others — but these are only described in minor or tangential ways (Meyers 1998, 252).

In addition to being androcentric, the Hebrew Bible, like many other ancient Near Eastern texts, is a formal text, an official document that does not represent the daily lives of the masses; thus, "there is a gap between what the documents depict and what happens in real life" (Meyers 2008, 252). For example, we cannot assume that all of the laws mandated in the Hebrew Bible were actually followed during the Iron Age, which is important when one considers, for example, the effects that the purity laws described in Leviticus may or may not have had on the daily lives of ancient Israelite women (Chapters 3 and 5). There are other challenges involved in the use of the Hebrew Bible and texts from the ancient Near East and Egypt (which were used to a lesser degree in my research), and one must carefully consider the limitations of using ancient textual sources to inform on the daily lives of women.

Iconography

Iconographic, or representational, sources from the ancient world are important for understanding aspects of women's lives in ancient Israel, although, admittedly, very few iconographic representations have been found in the Iron I villages themselves. Most of the images used here date to the succeeding Iron Age II (c. 1000–586 BCE) or are among the art of Israel's neighbors, and they may not accurately reflect the lives of the Iron I highland population.

A more fundamental problem concerning the availability of representational art is the fact that ancient Israel was purportedly an aniconic culture,[10] and perhaps as a result very few images of men have been found in Iron Age Israelite or Judean contexts. However, the same is not true of female images, as there are well over a thousand known female pillar figurines that may depict actual women or a goddess (Chapter 6) that date to the Iron Age II.

Other images of females from the art of Israel and Judah, as well as that of the neighboring Phoenicians and the Assyrians, appear throughout this book in the figures; they include such images as a woman kneading dough (Figure 2.1), a woman bathing (Figure 3.1), a woman playing a hand drum (Figure 4.1), women from Lachish being led into exile (Figure 4.2), a pregnant woman (Figure 5.1) and a woman mourning (Figure 7.1). These images may inform on such things as women's dress and appearance in ancient Israel as well as some of the activities in which women were engaged. Since these figurines, models and wall reliefs do not offer insights into most of the daily life activities discussed in this book, we must look to Egypt, where abundant iconographic depictions of women performing various household and field tasks are known, to help us reconstruct female crafts, technologies and other activities in the past. One must keep in mind that Egyptian representations of women reflect Egyptian artistic conventions, ideology and attitudes toward women and do not necessarily reflect the reality of their daily life experiences in Egypt or elsewhere.

Ethnography

Ethnographic and ethnoarchaeological[11] sources comprise the final category of material used to reconstruct women's lives in ancient Israel. Meyers asserts that "[c]urrent archaeological interpretation is inevitably ethnoarchaeological and, therefore, comparativist in its approach" (Meyers 1997, 277), a statement that betrays archaeologists' reliance on the present when reconstructing the past. Indeed, the earliest studies of the form and function of Israelite houses (i.e. Holladay 1992; Stager 1985) were informed by ethnographic research conducted in the Middle East. This research, performed and published by female anthropologists working in Iran in the 1970s and 1980s, is now considered among the classic works of rural Middle Eastern villages that archaeologists continue to cite (Meyers 2002a, 21). When investigating aspects of ancient Israel, the most useful and appropriate comparative material must come from societies that are similar to ancient Israel in various ways; as Meyers notes (2003a, 430), there is more possibility of cultural continuity if one uses data from the same geographic region. Since geography, climate and agricultural potential were critically important in the lives of the Iron I villagers, I found the research conducted in Palestine to be most useful in my research of this book.[12]

Ethnographic documentation from nineteenth- and early twentieth-century Palestine thus provided much information on female participation in specific domestic and field activities. Other ethnographic sources that I consulted include ethnographic information from nineteenth- and twentieth-century Egypt and contemporary studies of Middle Eastern (Sephardic) women living in modern Israel. Using ethnographic sources to shed light on cultural practices and traditions like marriage patterns, childbirth customs and the like in antiquity is more difficult, but when used along with ethnohistoric sources like the Hebrew Bible, these data may provide useful information for reconstructing past activities. However, most early ethnographers in this region were men who were neither interested in nor privy to the lives of women living in traditional Muslim and Christian societies, and their primary goal was often to illustrate the biblical stories by recording the customs of those living in the same region. As a result, some of their descriptions and sketches are fanciful if not completely wishful thinking.

Most useful for this book have been the extensive published records of Finnish anthropologist Hilma Granqvist, who spent years documenting the lives of the people of Artas, a village near Bethlehem, in the first half of the twentieth century (Granqvist 1931, 1935, 1947). Her access to female villagers and her interest in their lives, along with the assistance of Louise Baldensperger, Granqvist's English-speaking host and interpreter who lived in the village and knew the people and culture well, make these sources particularly useful. Although there is certainly no one-to-one correspondence between the lives of women living in Palestine less than a century ago and those of the Iron I village population, the descriptions of women's everyday activities in a rural, largely self-sufficient village in very close proximity to the ancient geographical setting of this book were quite helpful in my research. Perhaps more importantly, these sources gave me a new appreciation of and respect for women's myriad and overwhelming economic responsibilities in traditional agrarian households, as well as their critical roles in the preservation of family customs and traditions.

All four sources discussed above have their strengths and weaknesses, but all proved invaluable in my reconstruction of women's lives in biblical times and each was utilized to varying extents in this book. Although I do not attempt to provide a comprehensive account of what we can know of women's lives according to the available sources, as this is beyond the scope of a book that endeavors to be accessible to a wide audience, the reader is urged to consult the sources in the Bibliography to learn more about specific topics of interest.

The Historical Context

In order to provide historical context for the events described in this book, including elements of Orah's (fictional) story, I will now very briefly discuss the events leading up to the Iron Age I period in the Late Bronze Age, give an account of what occurred in the southern Levant during Israel's formative period in the Iron Age I and describe the events immediately following, in the Iron Age II. I will also explain why I have chosen to set this book in the Iron Age I period.

Orah's story is set in a dynamic period in the history of the eastern Mediterranean called the Iron Age I or early Iron Age by archaeologists and others working in this region. This approximately 200-year period (c. 1200–1000 BCE) witnessed the movement of several groups of people in the southern Levant and the settlement of a region that had previously been rather sparsely settled: the central highlands. Corresponding roughly to the eastern part of the Palestinian territories, also known as the West Bank, this central spine west of the Jordan River was the main setting of the events during Israel's formative period after the Exodus as described in the books of Joshua and Judges in the Hebrew Bible. Although there is no direct correspondence between these textual accounts and the history of this region as reconstructed from archaeological excavations at Iron I sites, many scholars believe that accounts in Judges can inform on the lifeways of the population of the central highlands during this time.

Late Bronze Age (c. 1550–1200 BCE)

During the previous period, called the Late Bronze Age (c. 1550–1200 BCE), much of the southern Levant — which during the Bronze Age is called Canaan — was occupied by the New Kingdom (c. 1550–1069 BCE) pharaohs of neighboring Egypt. Egypt was the dominant power in this part of the world at the time, and the only other serious threat to Egyptian preeminence came from the kings of the Hittite New Kingdom, who were based in Anatolia. Egyptian presence in the land is unmistakable, and there are abundant archaeological remains and Egyptian and Canaanite textual sources that inform on this period. Canaan was organized into city-states, and

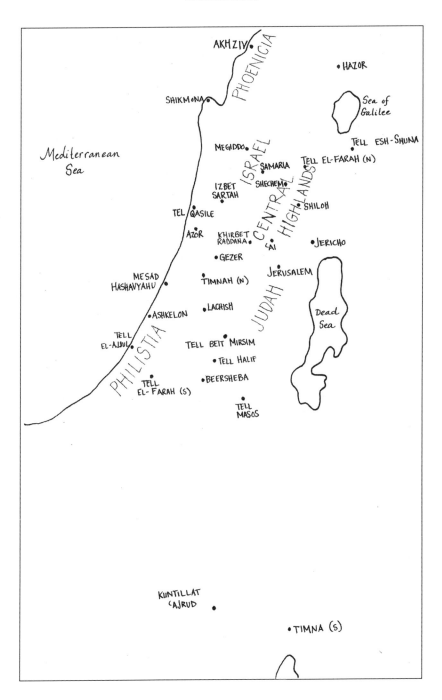

The Southern Levantine sites discussed in this book.

many city-states were ruled by a minor king or prince who appears to have been under the direct authority of the Egyptian crown. The cosmopolitan nature of the material culture, or artifacts, unearthed in Canaan during the Late Bronze Age bear witness to Canaan's role in international commerce with the kingdoms of the eastern Mediterranean, and the rich and complex religious traditions of the Canaanites and resident Egyptians are evident in the dozens of temples and shrines that date to this period. Temple remains, as well as the artifacts excavated from tombs, Egyptian governors' residences and, occasionally, Canaanite houses, demonstrate the wealth of the urban elites during the Late Bronze Age.[13]

In the thirteenth century BCE, groups of invaders and settlers originating mainly in the Aegean world and known as the "Sea Peoples" entered the eastern Mediterranean by land and sea and threatened Egypt and other kingdoms in the region. They were successfully repulsed by the Egyptians, who never permitted the settlement of the Sea Peoples in the Delta or elsewhere in the Egyptian homeland. Some groups of Sea Peoples were settled on the southern coast of Canaan; one group, the Peleset, known in the Bible as the Philistines, eventually founded a *pentapolis* (five cities) and other settlements in the region. The Sea Peoples' presence weakened Egypt to the point that it lost control of Canaan sometime after 1200 BCE. Sea Peoples are believed to have destroyed the capital of the Hittites, Hattusha, as well as the capital cities of other kingdoms along the Syrian and Levantine coast and on Cyprus around this time.[14] Many Canaanite cities were destroyed as well.[15]

Iron Age I (c. 1200–1000 BCE)

These movements of people and destructions of cities resulted in massive disruptions throughout the Mediterranean world, including Canaan. As part of this process, it appears that part of the urban Canaanite population and other social elements, like the 'Apiru known from the Amarna Letters, refugees and local pastoral nomads (Dever 2003, 181–82), fled to the relatively empty region of the central highlands and founded new villages.[16] Meanwhile, groups of Sea Peoples settled the coast and the Egyptians continued to occupy several strongholds in the land. Hundreds of small, undefended settlements founded during the twelfth century BCE have been surveyed or excavated in the central highlands, and some aspects of the material culture at these sites show continuity with that of the Late Bronze Age Canaanites.[17] There is limited evidence of social stratification or the presence of elites in these settlements, and those who lived in the most isolated hilltop villages were self-sufficient (see Chapter 1).[18]

This appears to be the setting of Israel's formative period described in the books of Joshua and Judges in the Hebrew Bible, and many attempts have been made to use the biblical text to discuss the Israelite settlement or conquest of Canaan after the Exodus. Most archaeologists do not accept the account of wholesale conquest described in Joshua because it is not reflected in the archaeological remains,[19] but the account in Judges — which differs significantly from that in Joshua — accords with the archaeological data in various ways. Like Joshua, the book of Judges was composed at least several hundred years after the period it purports to describe, but most scholars believe that some of the material included in it was composed at an earlier date. Extra-biblical textual information for early Israel is found in the Merneptah stele, which dates to the end of the thirteenth century BCE. This inscription of the pharaoh Merneptah refers to "Israel" as a people or ethnic group, and the evidence suggests that the location of Merneptah's Israel is most likely the central highlands (Faust 2006, 164–65). Most archaeologists thus refer to the central highland settlers as Israelites or "proto-Israelites" in the Iron Age I, although it is possible that other ethnic groups settled this region as well (Faust 2006, 229).

Although a detailed discussion of the origins of the Iron I population is beyond the purview of this review,[20] suffice it to say that, despite their apparently heterogeneous origins, the highland settlers seem to have formed a cohesive group of agriculturalists by the late twelfth century BCE, sharing material culture, a common architectural style and similar adaptations to the harsh surroundings. Although evidence for minor altercations with neighboring groups is hard to identify archaeologically, and the general absence of defenses in the highland villages is notable, the locations of many settlements on isolated hilltops and the lack of imported items might hint to tensions with other ethnic groups. Later, in the eleventh century BCE, many of the inhabitants of the small villages moved to larger, more centrally located sites under pressure from the Philistines. This was an important factor in the consolidation of the highland population into a united kingdom (Faust 2006, 229).

The book of Judges describes the tensions that the Israelites faced with the neighboring Philistines as well as those Canaanites who continued to live in their Late Bronze Age cities and villages, and this is reflected in a minor way in this book. At the beginning of our story, Orah's father has taken in a refugee from the coast and she has already borne him a son, Orah's half-brother. Although I do not provide specific details of the concubine's background, I imagine that her father was a former Egyptian administrator still living on the coast as Egypt's hold on Canaan waned, and her mother was a Philistine whose coastal town was raided by Canaanites or highlanders who resisted the Sea Peoples' presence. Although this scenario is entirely imagined, it is inspired by the interesting mix of peoples living in a small region during a turbulent time as reflected in the archaeological remains and descriptions in the book of Judges. Two passages in Ezekiel — Ezekiel 16.3 and 16.45 — also refer to Israelite origins among the various groups that occupied the land before it was "settled" by Israel.[21] Orah's father's acceptance of this woman, with her foreign cultural and religious traditions, reflects the diverse origins of the highland settlers, of which Israel may have only been one group.

Specifically, Orah's story is set in the last 20 years of the twelfth century and first 20 years of the eleventh century BCE (c. 1120–1080 BCE), which corresponds to the period before the Ark of the Covenant was taken from the shrine at Shiloh according to 1 Samuel 4. Archaeological excavations at Shiloh have shown that the Iron I site was at its peak of prosperity in the first half of the eleventh century BCE (Finkelstein 1993, 386–89), even if no direct evidence for the shrine containing the Ark was found there. In the story, Orah first sees her future husband on the pilgrimage to Shiloh (Chapter 4) and later makes the pilgrimage to Shiloh with her family in part to celebrate the weaning of her youngest child (Chapter 6). This 40-year period also corresponds to the time when Philistine bichrome (two-colored) ware — the pottery that Orah watches the concubine decorate when she is a young girl (Chapter 2) — was likely made and used in Philistia. It also dates to the period just after the reign of pharaoh Rameses III (1186–1155 BCE), when Egypt's hold on Canaan was lost (Killebrew 2005).

Iron Age II (c. 1000–586 BCE)

According to 1 and 2 Samuel, the Israelite tribes were united by a series of leaders whose roots were in the central highlands, beginning with Saul. The period of the United Monarchy of Israel (dated by most archaeologists to c. 1000–925 BCE) witnessed the reigns of David, who is credited with conquering and establishing a capital city at Jerusalem and expanding the kingdom of Israel to its greatest geographical extent, and his son Solomon, whose reign led to the breakup of Israel into two entities — Israel in the north and Judah in the south — around 925 BCE. Other tribal groups, including Ammon, Moab and Edom in Transjordan, coalesced into monarchies in the tenth century as well, while the Philistines continued to occupy the southern coastal area. The Phoenicians, descendants of the coastal-dwelling Canaanites of the Bronze Age, occupied the northern coastal areas during this time. Archaeology of the tenth century BCE reflects a period of reurbanization in the southern Levant, evidenced by the construction of three royal cities outside of the capital of Jerusalem, at Hazor, Megiddo and Gezer, with their palaces, public buildings and fortification systems.

As these and other cities were founded on the remains of former Canaanite strongholds, the remaining population of the central highlands abandoned this inhospitable region to settle in new urban centers or in rural areas with greater potential for agricultural success. The Deuteronomistic history recorded in the books of 1 and 2 Kings and the records of the Chronicler preserved in 1 and 2 Chronicles provide an outline of the events that took place in the kingdoms of Israel (c. 925–721 BCE) and Judah (c. 925–586 BCE) until Israel was destroyed at the hands of the Assyrians and Judah by the Babylonians and parts of the population were dispersed. Numerous extrabiblical sources inform on this period as well. The entire period of the Israelite monarchy, which corresponds to the Iron Age II (c. 1000–586 BCE), is perhaps the best-known archaeological period in the history of the region (Herr 1997, 115).[22]

Why the Iron Age I?

Some believe that Iron I society was more egalitarian — that is, everyone was essentially equal — than that of the succeeding Iron Age II. Although I do not necessarily agree that Iron I society was egalitarian (see further Chapter 1), I do accept other scholars' suggestions that women played particularly vital roles in their households and communities during the Iron Age I (Ackerman 2003, 175–77; Meyers 2002a, 28–33; Meyers 2003a, 435–37). Carol Meyers has shown in her analyses of women's control of food (2002a, 2003a) and textile production (2003a) that women gained power in their households and communities through bread making and cloth production (Meyers 2003a, 435); this power may have also accrued to women who produced beer for their households (Ebeling and Homan 2008). As I discuss in this book, women controlled many other crafts and technologies that were necessary in their largely self-sufficient communities. Women's critical roles in the household economy are what drew me to set this book during Israel's formative period.

The descriptions of women in the book of Judges seem to support this picture of women as essential parts of their communities. As Susan Ackerman notes, there are more major female characters in Judges than in any other biblical book except for Genesis, and these women "are depicted as fulfilling the exact sorts of economic, social, political, and religious roles within their communities that Meyers' examination of the archaeological, sociological, and ethnographic data available for the Iron I period predicts" (Ackerman 2003, 176). Deborah is the parade example of an important female character in Judges. According to Judges 5, which most biblical scholars believe to date to c. 1100 BCE (Ackerman 2003, 177), Deborah was Israel's chief military commander and was chosen by Yahweh to sound the war leader's cry to summon Israel's troops into battle. Ackerman asks if it was possible for the biblical writers to describe a female military leader during this time because women in Iron I Israel were participants or even leaders in military engagements (Ackerman 2003, 177). Even if this was not the case, Deborah's preeminence in Judges may indicate that women had other important responsibilities in their communities in addition to their control of household subsistence activities and technologies.

Summary of Chapters

Seven chapters comprise the remainder of this book. Each chapter is prefaced with a brief narrative account of Orah's life at a specific age and in a different time of year, and the rest of the chapter provides a scholarly discussion of the events described in the narrative. Four major topics related to women's daily experiences that are also relevant to Orah's age and the specific agricultural season are discussed in detail in each chapter.

Chapter 1 provides an introduction to the Israelite family and the Iron Age I village into which a baby girl named Orah is born. It focuses on the locus of family life — the four-room house and its associated outdoor spaces — and provides details of the diet and economy of the extended family (the *bet 'ab* or *bet 'em*) and the agricultural cycle by which they live. This chapter is set in spring during the barley harvest, which was celebrated with the *pessah/ massot* festival.

Chapter 2 focuses on the experiences in the life of Orah when she is eight years old. During this time she learns the most important domestic skills she will need in her future roles of wife and mother: baking bread and brewing beer, making pottery and spinning thread and weaving textiles. This chapter also briefly summarizes the evidence for the education and literacy of girls during this time and highlights the important role that women played in the education of their daughters. This chapter is set at the end of the barley and wheat harvest, when Orah's favorite annual holiday — *shevuot* — was celebrated.

Chapter 3 includes a discussion of the events that may have surrounded Orah's transition to womanhood at age 12. In this chapter, Orah is instructed on how to handle her first menstruation and experiences the partial isolation from male household members that she and the other women in her household practice during this time. She joins the women of her household, including her older sister Adah, in making offerings to the goddess Astarte and receives special perfume to mark her introduction to the world of women. This chapter is set in early summer, when early grapes are harvested and wine produced.

In Chapter 4, Orah is 15 years old and her parents have chosen a slightly older man from a nearby village for her to marry. Wedding arrangements and customs, including Orah's move to her new husband's village several hours' walk away, are described. Music and dancing accompany the wedding festivities in Orah's village and the village of her husband, and these are discussed along with clothing and adornment. This chapter is set in midsummer, when pomegranates (potent fertility symbols in ancient Israel), dates and other summer fruits ripen in the terraces surrounding Orah's birth village and the village of her husband.

Chapter 5 describes the birth of Orah's first child at age 18. The birth is accompanied by a midwife and female family members of Orah's husband's household, and it involves a number of ritual activities performed by the midwife and the other women, including the use of spells, incense and amuletic jewelry. The technology of basketry is discussed in this chapter as well, as Orah makes a woven cradle for her new son out of locally available materials during the long final weeks of her pregnancy. This chapter takes place in late summer, when the last of the pomegranates and figs are harvested.

In Chapter 6, a month in Orah's adult life is described when she is 26 years old. By this time a woman in ancient Israel may have given birth many times and had two or three surviving children; Orah's son is now eight years old, and her daughter, Hilah, is three. Breastfeeding and weaning practices are described in this chapter, and Orah has just weaned her little daughter before the family is to travel to Shiloh on the annual pilgrimage to Yahweh's shrine. Hide working is also discussed, and Orah produces several leather items that she will offer to the priests at the shrine. This chapter is set in the early fall, when olives are harvested and the pilgrimage to the shrine at Shiloh takes place around the time of the 'asip/sukkot festival.

The last chapter, Chapter 7, describes Orah's final days. Orah is in her late thirties, old enough to know a grandson. She lives in the same house she shared with her deceased husband, only now her son is the head of the household. This chapter discusses attitudes toward widowhood and provides an overview of health and medical practices during this period. Orah contracts an infection in her broken leg that cannot be cured by the members of her household or a wise woman from a nearby village, and she dies after being nursed by her daughter Hilah for several days. On the day of her death, the women of the household handle her body and perform various funerary rituals before she is buried in the cemetery on the outskirts of the village. Her surviving family members preserve Orah's memory through a mortuary cult for a while, and young women hoping to conceive visit her grave with the hope that her spirit will help them; eventually, however, her progeny leave the village and settle in the urban centers that develop throughout the land and her tomb is forgotten. This chapter takes place in the cold and rainy early winter, when the fields are sown with the barley and wheat that will be harvested in the following spring.

Notes

1   See, for example, Bach, ed. 1998; Bellis 1994; Frymer-Kensky 2004; Meyers, Craven and Kraemer, eds. 2000; Newsom and Ringe, eds. 1998; Trible 1984.

2   An important exception is Carol L. Meyers, a biblical scholar and archaeologist who has pioneered the study of women in ancient Israel using multiple sources of evidence. Meyers has written numerous articles and book chapters on this topic before and since the publication of her seminal work *Discovering Eve: Ancient Israelite Women in Context* in 1988, and this book is informed throughout by her many important contributions to the study of women in biblical times.

3   See, for example, Ackerman 1989, 1992; Bird 1997; Hadley 2000; Meyers 2002b, 2005; Willett 1999, 2008.

4   See further Ackerman 2003 for a recent history of the study of biblical women by feminist biblical scholars.

5   A very interesting fictional ethnography set in an Iron Age I village has also recently been published that focuses on Israelite religious life (van der Toorn 2003).

6   See, among others, Burton 2005a, 2005b, 2006a, 2006b; Card 2001, 2002, 2005; Edghill 2002, 2004; Etzioni-Halevy 2005, 2007, 2008; Halter 2005, 2006, 2007.

7   The fictional works in part stimulated my own interest in this project, so it is fair to say that they, like the academic sources, have their place in attempts to reconstruct the lives of biblical women.

8   I use the *HarperCollins Study Bible: New Revised Standard Version* (1993) in this book.

9   Syria-Palestine refers to the western, coastal portion of the ancient Near East or modern Middle East; the term is meant to be politically "neutral" as it makes no reference to modern political entities. This area is also called the Levant. The southern Levant corresponds to the modern state of Israel, the Palestinian territories and Jordan.

10   The second commandment given in Exod. 20.4 and Deut. 5.8 forbids the making of

images, although the biblical writers describe the Israelites making and using idols (Isa. 30.22). It seems that images of the male deity were expressly forbidden, while images from nature, like the cherubim in the Jerusalem Temple, were at times permitted (King and Stager 2001, 131).

11 Ethnoarchaeology is ethnographic research carried out by archaeologists who have specific archaeological questions or problems in mind. It has been particularly useful for archaeologists investigating ancient crafts and technologies, like pottery production. See further Carter 1997.

12 Very few ethnoarchaeological studies have been conducted in Palestine/Israel by archaeologists for the specific purpose of explaining Bronze and Iron Age phenomena.

13 For a brief introduction to the Late Bronze Age, see Leonard 2003. Lengthier, although somewhat outdated, discussions of the period can be found in Gonen 1992, Leonard 1989 and Mazar 1992.

14 See Killebrew 2005 for more information on what happened in the Levant c. 1300–1100 BCE.

15 See Dever 2003 for a recent summary of sites destroyed at the end of the Late Bronze Age.

16 Faust includes in this group "a semi-nomadic population who lived on the fringe of settlement, settled Canaanites who for various reasons changed their identity, tribes from Transjordan, and probably even a group who fled Egypt. In the end it is likely that many, if not most, Israelites had Canaanite origins" (2006, 186).

17 Many scholars continue to stress continuity between the material culture of the Late Bronze Age and that of the Iron Age I. Although Late Bronze Age pottery forms persist into the Iron Age I, Faust 2006 shows that many aspects of Iron I material culture and architecture — including the limited pottery repertoire, lack of imported and decorated pottery, simple burials, lack of temples and others — actually differ quite a bit from that of the Late Bronze Age Canaanites, however (227–28).

18 See Bloch-Smith and Nakhai 1999 for more on the Iron Age I.

19 Bloch-Smith and Nakhai write, "Were it not for the Bible, no late thirteenth-early twelfth century Israelite invasion would be suspected" (1999, 118).

20 See Dever 2003 and Faust 2006 for recent, detailed discussions of Israel's origins.

21 Ezekiel 16.3 states "... your father was an Amorite, and your mother a Hittite" and Ezekiel 16.45 reads "... your mother was a Hittite and your father an Amorite."

22 See Herr 1997 and Younker 2003 for more on the Iron Age II.

Chapter 1
Birth and Background

The baby girl did not yet comprehend what was happening around her, but she was already an important member of her household just the same. A healthy newborn, her life was a cause for celebration, but it was understood that danger always lurked and this new and precious life could be taken in an instant. She had already been given the name Orah — *light*[1] — by her mother with the hope that it would help deflect the dark forces that always threatened. Orah's mother wore an amulet around her neck for protection and many prayers had already been uttered during and after the birth, but Orah's mother believed in and respected the power of names; only a few months earlier her sister-in-law's baby had died during birth, and Orah's mother thought that extra protection might be needed in their household. Orah's birth was considered particularly auspicious because it occurred just after the *massot* festival that celebrated the spring barley harvest. Perhaps Yahweh, the primary male god worshiped in Orah's house, would find special favor with this child and help protect her from harm.

This was the third time Orah's mother had given birth, and she had one other surviving child, a three-year-old daughter named Adah.[2] Orah's mother had come to her husband's village about five years earlier, and shortly after the wedding her father-in-law had died, leaving her husband the senior male member of the household. Twelve people now lived in the two-story house: Orah, her parents and sister; Orah's widowed grandmother; a young unmarried uncle; and another, married uncle, his wife and their two sons. Her father's concubine, who had come to the village several years earlier when Orah's mother was pregnant with Adah, and her young son completed the house-hold. The concubine was a refugee from a town on the coast of the Great Sea. She brought unfamiliar customs to the village, and it took some time before the members of Orah's mother's household, especially the women, accepted her as part of their extended family. The concubine worshiped some of the same deities as the women in the household, however, and her status

23

increased greatly after she gave birth to a son two years before.

Three days after Orah's birth, her mother was up and walking about the house a bit during the daytime while most of the members of her family were in the fields, occupied with the barley harvest. Her mother-in-law — who had stayed behind to help with the new baby — begged her to lie down and take advantage of this rare opportunity to rest while the baby slept, but Orah's mother needed the air and light of the courtyard after spending several days in a windowless room in the rear of the house. She fingered the blue beads and the small figurine strung on a cord around her neck while she walked into the courtyard accompanied by her mother-in-law and daughter Adah, and was cheered by the familiar sights in the village and beyond. In the distance, on a hilltop higher than that on which her village sat, Orah's mother could just make out the village where her husband traded grain and olive oil for tools and other items. Much closer to home, she could see the barley sheaves piled on the threshing floor located on a terrace close to the village. From her courtyard she could also see several of the seven other houses in the village and observe the older women and young children moving about their compounds. A few of the neighbor women, whom she knew very well, made gestures of blessing to Orah's mother and her house.

After chatting with Adah under the shelter in the courtyard while drinking a bowl of cool water, Orah's mother decided to check on Orah, who was sleeping in a rear room of the house in a woven basket set upon a mat on the dirt floor. As Orah's mother entered the house, she paused for a moment just inside the doorway where a low mudbrick bench stood under a shallow niche carved into the mudbrick wall; several clay figurines were propped up inside the niche, along with a small pile of shells and some bluish pebbles that protected the family, the house, and the new baby from harm. In a low voice she murmured a prayer of thanks to the gods that protected her and her children, and she asked Adah to bring a handful of new barley from a jar inside the house to place on the bench altar. As she did so, Adah looked reverently at the gods in the niche above, while her mother smiled at the little girl's youthful sincerity.

As they entered the house, Orah's mother surveyed the spaces she had come to know intimately since her arrival five years before. Just in front of her was the main room of the house, which was divided by two rows of stone pillars that supported a second story. The two long side rooms formed by the pillars were paved with stones and served as stables for her household's livestock in bad weather and storage during the rest of the year. The main room, although used for many purposes, was sometimes a food preparation area and it contained tools and cooking installations including sets of grinding stones, a hearth and an oven. At the rear of the ground floor were two more small rooms: the room on the left was where Orah was born and where she now slept, and the room on the right was a storage room that contained grain, wine and oil stored in ceramic jars of varying sizes, cooking and serving vessels and other assorted utensils. A ladder placed against the row of pillars on the left led to the upper story, where bedding and clothing were stored and where a loom stood propped against an outer wall. Since the heat and smoke from the main room rose to the second floor, no one spent much time up there after the cooler morning hours; now that the weather was pleasant, much of the daily food processing and weaving activities were carried out under the courtyard shelters.

Orah's mother entered the left rear room — the west room — to nurse Orah as she started to stir, and she was soon dozing on the mat next to her baby in the heat of the afternoon. She intermittently heard the activity in the courtyard and in the main room just beyond the thin mudbrick wall as the women and younger children returned from a day spent harvesting in the fields to prepare the evening meal for the men, who would return later. Just before dark, when the men returned from the threshing floor, everyone ate the evening meal in the coolness of the courtyard while they talked about the work they had done that day and made plans for the next. After the children were put to sleep on mats spread on the roof and while the men repaired their tools in the light of the hearth in the main room, Orah's mother brought Orah into the courtyard so that they could relax in the cool evening air with the rest of the women. As they sat under the stars, Orah's grandmother said a prayer of thanks to the goddess Astarte for the fertility of her sons and their wives, and Orah's mother hugged her little swaddled daughter close to her chest and said her own silent prayer of thanks.

Introduction

Orah is the name of a woman who might have lived in a time when charismatic leaders called Judges lived in the central highlands of ancient Israel, before much of the region in the southern Levant between the Mediterranean Sea and the Jordan River valley was ruled by kings. Although we can reconstruct some of the events in her life from the stories in the Hebrew Bible, Orah herself does not feature in them; instead, she was an average woman who lived a typical life in her father's, husband's and, finally, son's house for nearly 40 years. Information about what Orah's daily existence might have been like can be pieced together from the Hebrew Bible

(Old Testament), archaeological excavations and surveys of villages dating to the early Iron Age, or Iron Age I (c. 1200–1000 BCE), in Israel, textual references and iconographic depictions from neighboring cultures in the Near East and Egypt and ethnographic sources from nineteenth- and early twentieth-century CE Palestine and other areas in the modern Middle East. Although we can never know certain details of Orah's life, these sources provide enough information to tell part of her story and thus shed light on certain aspects of women's lives during the early Iron Age.

The village in which Orah is born is not based on a specific village described in the Hebrew Bible or revealed through archaeological excavations; it instead reflects a composite of what we know of the layout, architecture and artifacts uncovered at a number of small settlements excavated in the central highlands that date to the Iron Age I period. Orah's village was small, comprised of eight houses and their associated outdoor spaces and perched on a low hilltop surrounded by agricultural terraces. A larger village was located about an hour's walk away, but Orah's mother had only been there a few times; generally, the men in her household, including her husband, traveled to this village to trade surplus agricultural products for tools and other necessities a few times per year. Shiloh, a place visited at least once per year by Orah's entire family, was more distant; Shiloh was the site of sacrifices and an annual feast held in honor of Yahweh, the biblical god of Israel, whose portable sanctuary (Tabernacle) stood in Shiloh during the period when Orah would have lived (Josh. 18.1) (see Chapter 6). The most important object kept in the Tabernacle — the Ark of the Covenant — was taken by the Philistines and the shrine at Shiloh was destroyed soon after (1 Sam. 4.3-5, 10-11).

Most, but not all, of the people in Orah's village are related by blood; they form what the biblical text refers to as a *mishpaha*, or kinship group of related families that shared common settled space and worked the fields and orchards surrounding their village (Meyers 1997, 13). Although the number of people in the early Iron Age *mishpahot* (pl.) could vary widely, the size of Orah's *mishpaha* — about 100 souls — is within the range of what one would expect in an Iron Age I village. The *mishpaha* was divided into household units, or joint-family households (Schloen 2001, 150–55); each of the eight household units in Orah's village had its own two-story house with an attached outdoor area, while in other, similar villages household units could comprise several houses attached by a common courtyard. In the Hebrew Bible, the household unit is called the *bet 'ab* and it was the basic unit of Israelite society.

Bet 'Ab and Bet 'Em

The *bet 'ab*, literally "father's house," was composed of blood relatives as well as women connected through marriage. In addition to the nuclear family of two parents and their unmarried children, the *bet 'ab* might include several generations of family members, as well as slaves, servants and many others (King and Stager 2001, 39–40). The complexity of the *bet 'ab* is illustrated in the story of Micah in Judges 17; in the story, a Levite, a priest of the tribe of Levi, is hired by Micah to oversee the household cult and becomes in effect a member of Micah's *bet 'ab*, like a son to Micah (Judg. 17.11).

The *bet 'ab* refers not only to the members of the family, but also its economic aspect, and it included household structures, property and animals as well as people. Evidence for this can be seen in the Tenth Commandment, which provides a definition of the Israelite household: "You shall not covet your neighbor's house; you shall not covet your neighbor's wife, or male or female slave, or ox, or donkey, or anything that belongs to your neighbor" (Exod. 20.17). Thus "family household" might be a preferable translation for *bet 'ab*, because it takes into consideration the various functions of the household, including economic production, social activity, cultic — or religious — practices and more (Meyers 1991, 41).

Orah's family is typical for the Iron Age in that it is dynamic as well as multigenerational. Her father has lived his entire life in the same house; a few years before Orah's birth, he had become the senior male in the *bet 'ab* when his own father died. Other members of the household include Orah's widowed grandmother, her uncle and his family, and another unmarried uncle; in addition to Orah's immediate family, Orah's father also had a concubine with one young son. Since marriage arrangements in ancient Israelite society were patrilocal — married women went to live with their husband's family — the only adult women living in the household besides Orah's widowed grandmother are the women married or otherwise bound to her father and uncle. Since descent was patrilineal, or reckoned through the father, inheritance passed through the father's line, and having sons was critical to pass on the land inheritance, the *nahala*. The importance of the *nahala* made it acceptable for a man to take another wife or attempt to have a son by some other means, including through a female slave (Gen. 16.1-3) or even a prostitute (Judg. 11.1) (Bird 1997, 26).

Orah's father's concubine was a refugee from a distant town on the shore of the Mediterranean Sea; her father's family was Egyptian and her mother was a Philistine. Egypt controlled much of the southern Levant during the previous period, the Late Bronze Age (c. 1550–1200 BCE), and many

Egyptians continued to live in towns along the coast during the early Iron Age; the Philistines, a group of the Sea Peoples with Aegean origins, had settled on the southern Levantine coast around 1200 BCE. Polygyny — when a man has more than one wife — was practiced in early Israel, as many biblical passages attest. Later, during the period of the Israelite monarchy, monogamy became the standard and divorce was apparently more frequent (Bird 1997, 25). Some of the concubine's customs were different from those of the villagers, for instance, her method of decorating the pottery she skillfully made for the household (see Chapter 2), but she was well integrated into the *bet 'ab* by the time Orah was born.

Since descent and inheritance were generally reckoned through the father, the *bet 'ab* is usually considered to have been a patriarchal unit, with ultimate authority residing in the senior male of the household (King and Stager 2001, 36). However, there are problems applying the patriarchal model to ancient Israel, and passages in the Hebrew Bible attest to the primary roles of women in important family decisions and customs, such as marriage (see Chapter 4). Gender-based hierarchical structures, if they did exist at some level in ancient Israel, thus may not be at all applicable to the *bet 'ab* of the Iron Age I (Meyers 2006, 245–47). The evidence suggests that women had much power in the agriculturally-based villages of this period due to their great economic contributions to the household (see below). Thus heterarchy — a system in which an individual could be ranked in a number of different ways — might be a more appropriate expression of the social realities of Iron Age I villages (Meyers 2007).

The importance of women in the Israelite household might be seen in an expression that appears rarely in the Hebrew Bible: *bet 'em*, or "mother's house" (Gen. 24.28; Ruth 1.8; Song 3.4; 8.2). The four biblical passages that include the expression *bet 'em* share the same characteristics: a woman's story is being told; a wisdom association is present; women are agents in their own destiny; the agency of women affects others; the setting is domestic; and marriage is involved (Meyers 1991, 49). In addition, Proverbs 31, the "Woman of Valor" proverb, refers to *betah*, meaning "her house" or "her household" (Prov. 31.21, 27), as the context for this woman's participation and management of household tasks and responsibilities. The righteous woman described in the poem does not just run the household: she defines it (Camp 1985, 91).

The physical setting for the *bet 'ab* or *bet 'em* in early Israel was a household consisting of one or more housing units with a courtyard. In this story, Orah's *bet 'ab* of 12 individuals resides in a two-story house with a large outdoor courtyard in which many daily life activities are carried out. In Iron Age I

Israel the form of the house varied widely, but was based on a common plan of three or four rooms on the ground level with perhaps a second story. Despite the variances in layout and number of rooms on the ground floor, this type of house is commonly called the four-room house.

Four-Room House and Women's Space

Orah was born in a small room in the rear of the ground floor of a house on the edge of her village that may have looked something like the reconstructed house in Figure 1.1. Divided lengthwise by two rows of stone pillars, the lower

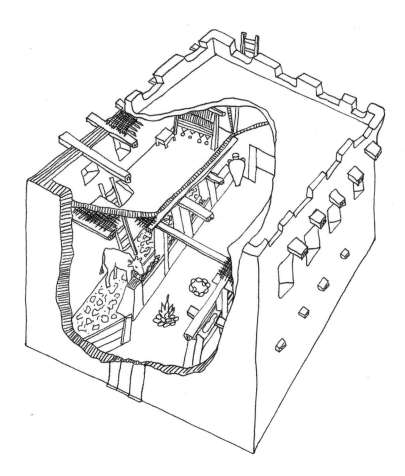

1.1 Four-room house (after King and Stager 2001, Ill. 15).

level was originally conceived as a four-room structure consisting of two long rooms to the left and right of the entrance, a central space in the middle and one broad room in the rear. The rear room had been divided into two rooms by a thin mudbrick wall and an upper story was added at some point in the house's history. The roof was also used for a variety of purposes, as was the courtyard, which was separated from the neighboring compounds by a low stone wall. Spaces within and outside of the house served various functions relating to the subsistence activities, religious practices and other habits of its occupants. Since women are believed to have been closely associated with the house and many of the activities performed in it during this period, women essentially controlled the use of space in and around Orah's house.

Some of the activities carried out on the lower story of Orah's house can be reconstructed using archaeological, biblical and ethnographic evidence. As is typical in four-room — or pillared — houses of the period, the floor of the lower story is partially paved and the rest is beaten earth. The paved portions correspond to the parts of the ground floor that were used during certain times of year for stabling animals; the rows of stone pillars separating these stables from the central space sometimes include stone troughs or mangers (Holladay 1992, 316). The central space had a few permanent installations built into it, all of them related to food preparation and storage: a hearth, a small oven and mud-plastered grain storage bins. A cistern for collecting and storing rainwater was dug into the bedrock below the floor of this main room as well. The west room in the rear of the house is the locus of a number of important activities in Orah's early life: it is where she is born, where she learns to worship the goddess Astarte upon her first menstruation (see Chapter 3) and where she witnesses other women in her household give birth. The small room next to it is primarily used for the storage of food and household implements.

Although they are not always easy to detect in archaeological excavations, upper stories and roofs are sometimes evidenced by the thickness of walls and the accumulation of building debris. In Orah's house, the second story provided a place for sleeping (1 Kgs 17.19; 2 Kgs 1.2; 4.11) and performing activities like spinning and weaving in the cold, rainy months. In addition, the woven bedclothes and mats used for sleeping were folded and stacked in piles on the upper floor along with most of the family's other personal belongings. The roof was used for sleeping in the hot summers and served many other functions as well. Use of roofs is suggested in Deut. 22.8: "When you build a new house, you shall make a parapet for your roof; otherwise you might have bloodguilt on your house, if anyone should fall from it." Evidence that the roof was used specifically for sleeping can be found in

1 Sam. 9.25, when a bed was spread on the roof for Saul. Ethnographic sources from early twentieth-century Palestine show that the roof was a multifunctional space that could be used as a storage place, a space for drying stalks and olives, an occasional fold for sheep and goats as well as a sleeping place in warm weather; women specifically used roof space to make storage jars and perform other household tasks (Wilson 1906, 69–70). The prostitute Rahab dried stalks of flax on the roof of her house in Jericho according to Josh. 2.6.

The origins of the four-room house, which appears as early as the late thirteenth–early twelfth century BCE, are still not fully understood. In the past, scholars focused on identifying the ethnic attribution of the house type (it was an Israelite creation) or its functional interpretation (it was well-suited to village agricultural life). This house form was non-standardized until the eleventh century (Faust 2006, 83) and, in the succeeding Iron Age II (c. 1000–586 BCE), most rural houses were of the four-room type while urban houses were smaller and belonged to a three-room subtype that may have housed nuclear families. The four-room house seems to have been an Israelite phenomenon, and its disappearance at the end of the Iron Age suggests that it served more than functional purposes: it may reflect aspects of Israelite ideology.

The size and layout of excavated four-room houses at Iron Age I sites are particularly suited to extended families, corresponding to the *bet 'ab* (Faust and Bunimovitz 2003, 26). This particular kind of layout may reveal cognitive aspects of the house plan, revealing how spatial configuration reflects such things as egalitarianism and privacy. Compared to houses in the preceding Late Bronze Age, the four-room house has a fairly open plan; in the earlier houses, access to certain rooms in the rear of the house might be restricted, but in the four-room house, one could enter many spaces from the large central room on the ground floor. This lack of "depth" in four-room houses might reflect a more egalitarian spirit or ethos than evidenced in earlier house plans in the southern Levant; it has long been speculated that the Iron Age I was a more egalitarian period compared to the hierarchical structures that developed during the succeeding Iron Age II.[3] In addition, the four-room house plan allowed for privacy, as it was possible to subdivide floor space on the ground floor as the family expanded. This could have accommodated Israelite purity laws — which may have imposed restrictions on women and others during states of impurity — or these later laws were structured by the house plan.

The importance of the household in Iron Age I villages has been high-lighted in recent research. According to Carol Meyers, "[t]he household is

. . . fundamental to human society because it is the level at which premodern social groups articulate directly with the environment in order to survive" (2003a, 426). Although the tribe is often considered to have been the primary social structure in the Iron I villages, it was really the household, "as the basic unit of production and reproduction," that was the primary socioeconomic unit of agrarian society (Meyers 2003a, 427). Women have traditionally been associated with the household or domestic sphere in ancient Israel; their contributions and experiences, however, have generally been considered less important than those of males, who participated in the public spheres of politics and Temple worship. But it is clear from ethno-graphic sources especially that self-sufficient agrarian households depend on the contributions of all family members. In early Israel, all the necessities of daily life, except for perhaps making metal implements, would have been the responsibility of both women and men (Meyers 1991, 41–42), with women and men contributing nearly equal amounts to household subsistence (Meyers 2007, 69).

However, most household tasks were carried out more often or exclu-sively by one of the sexes (Meyers 2007, 69). In ancient Israel, two of the most important productive activities performed primarily by women were food preparation — especially baking bread — and producing cloth (see Chapter 2). Thus, artifacts and installations related to these activities could represent the spaces used by women for at least several hours per day (Meyers 2003a, 430–32). Archaeological excavations have shown that these activities can be carried out in various indoor and outdoor spaces associated with the four-room house (see further Chapter 2); ethnographic sources from twentieth-century Palestine describe many female activities being carried out in courtyards in good weather. Women prepared food, washed dishes and clothes and performed other daily chores outdoors, and also used courtyard space for making pottery, baskets and other daily-use articles. The courtyard is described as an ideal playground for children, who could be watched easily while they were helping the women of the house with chores or simply playing (Amiry and Tamari 1989, 17–20). Many of these activities were carried out by women in Orah's courtyard in warm weather; in the cold and rainy winters, daily activities like cooking, baking bread and weaving took place indoors.

According to the ethnographic sources, courtyards were also important because they were spaces where "women carried out their daily work and mixed with female relatives or neighbours without inhibition or restriction" (Amiry and Tamari 1989, 17). It is possible that a similar situation existed in the Iron Age I, with groups of women working together on arduous, monotonous tasks like grinding grain or weaving in courtyard spaces. This may be evidence for the existence of women's networks in which women shared knowledge with one another while working together. Women may have gained power through their communal productive work, forming alliances through close associations with their neighbors (Meyers 2003a, 436). Women may have also gained social power in their households through their control of cooking activities, as the Israelite diet was maintained by the women responsible for provisioning their families with bread and other processed foods (Meyers 2002a, 30).

Diet and Economy

Agricultural production was the foundation of Iron Age I village economy, supplemented mainly through herding; thus we may assume that a family's wealth and power was based largely on its agricultural production capacity. The diet of the population of the central highlands was fairly simple and consisted almost entirely of food produced or raised locally. In this story, the main crops grown in the fields surrounding Orah's village are barley, wheat and lentils, and these carbohydrates are supplemented by vegetables grown in small garden plots and grapes, olives, pomegranates and figs grown on the agricultural terraces beyond the village. Orah's family's small herd of goats and sheep provide milk and cheese as well as materials for spinning, and the family owns two head of cattle that are used primarily for plowing. Meat itself is a rarity, and usually consumed on holidays. The care of the fields, gardens, terraces and animals was shared by all but the very youngest members of the household, and the division of tasks varied widely depending on the agricultural season.

The central highlands were sparsely settled during the preceding Late Bronze Age which is partly due to the fact that they lacked suitable agricultural land; the region is characterized by hilly terrain and valleys with few open fields. The challenges of producing field crops in the inhospitable environment of the central highlands were great, and the ancient Israelites learned to alter their environment in a number of ways for agricultural success, most importantly through clearing the land, developing strategies to store and divert rain water and building agricultural terraces. The hilltop on which Orah's ancestors established her village and the surrounding slopes were covered with bushes and thickets when the settlers arrived, and clearing was necessary before artificial terraces could be prepared for planting. Indeed, one of the first activities charged to the Israelites when they entered the land of Canaan was forest clearing (Josh. 17.14–18).[4] The relatively low rainfall in the region forced the village inhabitants to store water for their own use in cisterns and divert rain water to fields and terraces as well, although a perennial spring is located not far from Orah's village in our story.

The remains of ancient artificial terraces are abundant in this region, and although it is impossible to date most of them, their presence in areas with many Iron I villages suggests that at least some of them were constructed and used during this time. Scholars believe that building terraces required cooperative community participation, since terraces required a great deal of labor to build and maintain. Their benefits probably outweighed the high labor costs (Hopkins 1987, 184–85), since they were especially well suited to the cultivation of trees and vines, retained soil and helped to conserve rain water (King and Stager 2001, 87). Although they were not ideal for cultivating cereal grains, the villagers planted barley and wheat on some of the lower terraces as well as in the narrow valley beyond.

The terraces and fields surrounding Orah's village were sown with the staple crops of barley, wheat and lentils, and each household controlled a portion of these fields. Barley and wheat were sown in October–December but barley ripened earlier than wheat in the spring. The importance of both barley and wheat is seen in Deut. 8.8, which lists them among the seven crops and fruit trees with which the land was blessed (along with [grape] vines, figs, pomegranates, olive oil and honey). Archaeological remains of both barley and wheat have been excavated at sites in Israel dating to the Iron Age and earlier, as have the remains of storage silos, sickle fragments and ground stone tools used to process cereal grain for consumption. Legumes, too, were important in the ancient Israelite diet, and lentils could be sown in winter or spring for harvest in April or May.

Plowing and sowing could not begin until after the first rains had softened the ground in late fall or early winter. Plowing was a labor-intensive activity that was considered to be highly important, which is evident in the many biblical passages that use plowing metaphorically (Judg. 14.18; Isa. 2.4). Plows were machines made of wood that were attached to one or more draught animals – most often cattle or oxen – with a yoke. Each plow had an attached plow-share or point made of bronze or iron. After the plow was dragged over the ground, seeds could then be sown in the furrows by throwing them from bags or baskets. After the seeds were broadcast in the fields, they would be covered to protect them from birds and animals through plowing, by letting animals trample the area or by using a hoe (Borowski 2002, 47–54).

Harvesting cereals and legumes is a complex process that involves the use of a number of tools and technologies. The biblical text provides some details about these activities, and the remains of some of these tools have been recovered from archaeological excavations in Israel. Stalks of cereal grain were harvested by reapers using a sickle and the sheaves were collected, bound and stacked in piles in the fields. Sickles were made of wood or bone handles with sharpened flints embedded in them; although wood and bone rarely preserve, flint sickle blades have been found in archaeological contexts (Borowski 2002, 59–61). Iron sickle blades became available in Israel in the period of the monarchy, but flint sickle blades continued to be used by Palestinian farmers through the twentieth century CE. The sheaves were then transported by cart, animal or basket to a threshing floor located just beyond the village.

Once at the threshing floor, the main objective was to separate the grains of wheat from the stalks and collect the grains to take back to the house for storage. Threshing could be accomplished with a stick, with animals, a threshing sledge or with a wheel-thresher. The most common method during the Iron Age I was probably the threshing sledge, which was a wooden sled-shaped platform with sharp stones or pieces of iron embedded in its underside. The sledge was dragged by animals over the piled-up stalks, and it is possible that one or more people rode on the sledge to provide weight. Once the stalks were threshed, the material was thrown in the air (winnowed) with a large wooden winnowing fork. The wind would help separate the different materials so that the grain could be efficiently collected using sieves of various sizes. The other remaining material had various uses: straw could be used as kindling or in brick making, it could be fed to animals (Borowski 2002, 62–69) or it was collected by women to weave into mats and baskets (see Chapter 5).

Who participated in these field activities? Although the biblical evidence suggests that males were primarily responsible for harvesting and threshing, there are also textual descriptions of women performing these activities as well as many iconographic and ethnographic sources that demonstrate women's participation. During the busy harvest period, it is likely that every able-bodied person worked long days harvesting and processing the barley and wheat crops. During the harvests of barley and wheat (April to June) in Palestine in the 1970s and 1980s, "men reaped the crops using sickles, while women and older children gathered the sheaves and tied them into manageable bundles . . . Women and young girls also carried bundles on their heads as the whole family headed towards the village threshing floor" (Amiry and Tamari 1989, 35). Photographs from early twentieth-century Palestine show women and children harvesting cereals along with men.[5] According to Ruth 2.2, women gleaned the fields during harvest season.

Evidence that women participated in agricultural work can also be found in Egyptian art, where women are usually depicted with lighter skin than that of men unless they were lower-class women forced to work out in the fields. A biblical expression of this may be seen in Song 1.6: "Do not gaze at me because I am dark, because the sun has gazed on me. My mother's sons were angry with me; they made me keeper of the vineyards, but my own vineyard I have not kept!" In addition to participating in the spring cereal harvests, women in early Israel worked in the vineyards (see Chapter 3) and olive groves (see Chapter 6) in summer and fall. Other crops grown on the hillside terraces surrounding Orah's village include pomegranates and figs, which were harvested by the entire family in late summer.

Orah's household also maintained small vegetable gardens inside the walled courtyard and just outside of the village where they grew cucumbers, onions and spices. Very little archaeological evidence for these crops is available, although biblical passages suggest that a variety of vegetables and herbs were grown (Borowski 2003, 29); gardens were often located near houses (1 Kgs 21.2) and palaces (2 Kgs 21.18, 26) (Borowski 2002, 135–38). Cucumbers would have been desirable because of their high water content, and onions added flavor to cooked dishes and raw salads. Both are mentioned in Num. 11.5, but this passage refers to the cravings of the Israelites of the Exodus for the foods they had enjoyed in Egypt. Because small vegetable gardens do not require communal labor like the cultivation of large fields, each family cared for its own garden. The proximity of gardens to houses, where women presumably spent much of their time when not participating in seasonal work in the more distant fields, made gardening one of the tasks performed primarily by women. Since women's productive tasks had to be compatible with childcare, such gardening work occupied a significant part of women's outdoor time (Meyers 1998, 254).

This grain, fruit and vegetable-based diet was supplemented by dairy products made from the milk of the animals owned by each household. Orah's family's small herd of goats and sheep provided hair for making tents, sacks and ropes, and wool that could be woven into cloth in addition to milk for making yogurt, butter and hard cheese. Animal skins could also be used to make articles of clothing, containers for liquids and other items (see Chapter 6). The family's livestock was kept in pens constructed of field stones in the family compound in the warm season and housed indoors in the ground floor stables during the colder months, which provided extra heat in the house. The responsibility of their care fell mainly to the older children in the family, who pastured the animals when their help was not needed in the fields or at home. In the Hebrew Bible, young women are described as shepherds in several passages (Gen. 29.9; Song 1.8), and Orah helps her cousins shepherd the family's flock when she is a young girl (see Chapter 2).

Due to its expense, meat was a rare treat consumed at feasts and on other special occasions. Several biblical passages refer to serving meat to honor guests (Gen. 18.7-8; 1 Sam. 28.24-25) and describe the luxury of the diet of the royal court (1 Kgs 4.22-23) (King and Stager 2001, 68). In traditional small-scale agricultural societies, animals were valued for their so-called secondary products of milk, hair and labor, not for the meat that they could readily provide. When meat was desired, the Israelites killed one from among their sheep, goats or cows, or occasionally hunted wild animals; this is attested by both biblical passages and the animal bones recovered from archaeological excavations.[6] Deuteronomy 14.5 permits the consumption of wild animals like deer, gazelle and ibex, and several types of wild cattle were also consumed (Borowski 1998, 186–90). Fish was available in the Mediterranean Sea as well as in the lakes, rivers and streams of ancient Israel, but it was probably unavailable to most of the population of the central highlands.

The average village community was largely self-sufficient, and village inhabitants possessed very few imported objects beyond the heirlooms of previous generations and items brought by women who married into the families. There were few opportunities to acquire food or other items from beyond the village, although pilgrimages to shrines like the one at Shiloh (see Chapter 6) were times when special foods might be available, animals might be bought and sold, and crafts like textiles and pottery might be traded. Orah's village was typical by the standards of the day in that there was generally enough labor available for essential agricultural activities, negating the need for slaves and servants. Since agriculture was the foundation of their village economy, the *mishpaha* was fundamentally concerned with the agricultural cycle. Events related to the yearly agricultural cycle determined festival times and other celebrations; perhaps the most important for the Iron I village inhabitants was the spring barley harvest.

Agricultural Cycle

Since the agricultural seasons were key events in the lives of the highland villagers, in this story major events in Orah's lifecycle occur at specific times of year that correspond to the agricultural calendar and holiday celebrations. The traditional calendar with its cultic feasts is closely associated with agricultural life, and many of the Jewish holidays still celebrated today have their origins in the agricultural practices of the early Israelites. Orah's birth occurs at the start of the spring barley harvest — called *massot/pessah* — which was a major cause for celebration as well as one of the three most important festivals in the yearly cycle.

The earliest direct source of information about the Israelite agricultural calendar is the Gezer Calendar (Figure 1.2), which is a small inscribed limestone slab that is a kind of farmer's almanac. Found in excavations at Tel Gezer in the early twentieth century, this signed, seven-line tablet describes agricultural practices during the course of 12 months, beginning in the fall with the olive harvest. Seven more periods are described after the olive harvest: grain planting, late planting, hoeing, barley harvest, harvest and feasting, vine-tending and summer fruit (see further below) (King and Stager 2001, 87–88). Believed to date to the end of the tenth century BCE, just after the period when Orah would have lived, the Gezer Calendar may reflect the agricultural calendar of those living in the Iron Age I villages. The text uses

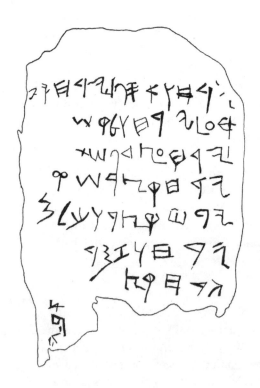

1.2 Gezer Calendar (after Dever 1993, 504).

the northern (Israelite) dialect and it may have been written just after the division of the kingdom, after the death of Solomon c. 922 BCE (Borowski 2002, 43–44).

The Hebrew Bible also mentions a number of agricultural activities and seasons at various times of year, but the biblical writers made no effort to present a complete agricultural calendar and it is thus not possible to establish precisely when each season began or ended (Borowski 2002, 31). Other information about the ancient Israelite calendrical system is given in occasional references to dates, days, months, seasons and years (Vanderkam 1992, 814). However, it is possible to estimate, using the information from the Gezer Calendar, the Hebrew Bible and data from modern agricultural practices in Israel, the approximate dates of agricultural festivals and corresponding agricultural activities.

Although the 12 periods described in the Gezer Calendar do not necessarily relate to exact months, it is possible to estimate the months in our calendar that correspond to the periods of each agricultural task. Lines 1 and 2 of the calendar describe the agricultural activities at the start of the Canaanite New Year: a period of two months of ingathering (of olives) in September and October, and two months of sowing (of barley and wheat) in November and December. This calendar thus reflects the tradition that the New Year began in the fall, in September. Line 2 continues with two months of late sowing of crops that probably include legumes and vegetables (January and February), and Line 3 relates that a month of hoeing weeds follows (March). Line 4 lists a month of harvesting barley in April, and Line 5 a month of harvesting wheat and feasting in May. Line 6 lists two months of grape harvesting in June and July, and Line 7 a month of gathering summer fruit in August.

Scholars have distinguished three dating systems for the religious festivals — *massot/pessah*, *shevuot* and *'asip/sukkot* — celebrated during the Iron Age II. The earliest calendrical system, and thus the one that would be most relevant in reconstructing the agricultural calendar of the Iron Age I population, is recorded in Exod. 23.14-18 and 34.18, 22-26. The second system — the Deuteronomic, or Holiness, calendar — appears in Deut. 16.1-4, 8 and lists the Deuteronomic reforms made by King Josiah no later than 609 BCE. The third system, which appears in Leviticus 23, was probably composed during the Babylonian Exile (beginning c. 586 BCE) or in post-exilic times (Borowski 2002, 38–39).

Originally *massot* and *pessah* were two separate festivals. According to the earliest biblical evidence, *massot* was celebrated for seven days beginning at the new moon of the month of *Abib*, and *pessah* — or Passover — was celebrated on the night preceding the start of *massot* (Exod. 23.14-15; Deut. 16.1) (Borowski 2002, 38–39). The Deuteronomic calendar maintains the same dates for these festivals, which suggests that they were celebrated throughout the period of the monarchy. The original intent of *massot/pessah* was the celebration of the beginning of the barley harvest, which corresponds to the month of April in our calendar.

The second major festival — called *hag haqqasir* (the Feast of the Harvest) in Exod. 23.16 and *hag shevuot* (the Feast of Weeks) in Exod. 34.22 — was celebrated seven weeks after *massot/pessah*, at the conclusion of the barley and wheat harvests. Some scholars believe that the weeks counted until *shevuot* began on the day after the completion of *massot*; according to the Hebrew Bible, it was to start ". . . seven weeks from the time the sickle is first put to the standing grain" (Deut. 16.9). *Shevuot* was the time when a portion of the harvest, a cereal offering, was made to Yahweh, and it is celebrated in our story when Orah is a young girl, in Chapter 2.

The last major festival, originally called *'asip* (Ingathering), was celebrated after the harvest of summer fruit, in September or October according to our calendar. The date of the festival was changed and it was renamed *sukkot* (Booths/Tabernacles) in the Priestly calendar. The feast was to last seven days and it marked the end of the agricultural — but not necessarily the calendar — year (Vanderkam 1992, 817). *'Asip/sukkot* was the period during which Solomon dedicated the Temple in Jerusalem (1 Kgs 8.63-65; 2 Chron. 7.8), and so this agricultural festival later took on a more religious meaning. Chapter 6 is set at this time of year, and in our story it is the time when Orah accompanies her husband and children on an annual pilgrimage to the sanctuary at Shiloh.

Did women participate in these festivals? According to Deut. 16.11, all are instructed to celebrate *shevuot*: "Rejoice before the Lord your God — you and your sons and your daughters, your male and female slaves, the Levites resident in your towns, as well as the strangers, the orphans, and the widows who are among you . . ." The same is said for *sukkot* in Deut. 16.13-14: "You shall keep the festival of booths for seven days, when you have gathered in the produce from your threshing floor and your wine press. Rejoice during your festival, you and your sons and your daughters, your male and female slaves, as well as the Levites, the strangers, the orphans, and the widows resident in your towns." Although the same is not clearly prescribed for *pessah*, it is implied that all are to celebrate this holiday (Deut. 16.1-8). All three of these holidays were special times for individual families and the community as a whole, as it was a time for giving thanks for agricultural success, visiting with family and friends and celebrating other important events, like the birth or weaning of a child. These celebrations would have thus strengthened families and communities in ancient Israel and given everyone something to look forward to during the difficult days of agricultural labor on which they relied.

For Further Reading

Borowski, O. 2003. *Daily Life in Biblical Times*. Atlanta: Society of Biblical Literature. A brief, accessible introduction to many aspects of daily life in ancient Israel that uses multiple sources of evidence. The final chapter is a narrative account of a day in the life of a family living in Judah during the Iron Age II.

Borowski, O. 2002. *Agriculture in Iron Age Israel*. Boston: American Schools of Oriental Research. A comprehensive discussion of agricultural practices in ancient Israel that relies on archaeological, biblical and other sources.

Borowski, O. 1998. *Every Living Thing: Daily Use of Animals in Ancient Israel*. Walnut Creek, CA: AltaMira Press. A study of the evidence for the cultic and secular use of animals in ancient Israel using multiple sources of evidence.

King, P.J. and L.E. Stager. 2001. *Life in Biblical Israel*. Louisville: Westminster John Knox Press. A well-illustrated and accessible handbook on life in ancient Israel that relies primarily on the biblical text. The authors include a brief narrative account of a day in the life of Micah's family (based on Judges 17–18) in the Introduction.

MacDonald, N. 2008. *What Did the Ancient Israelites Eat? Diet in Biblical Times*. Grand Rapids, MI: Eerdmans. A recent overview of the sources of evidence for the ancient Israelite diet.

Meyers, C.L. 1988. *Discovering Eve: Ancient Israelite Women in Context*. Oxford: Oxford University Press. The standard resource for women's lives in ancient Israel. In this groundbreaking study, Meyers uses social science models and archaeological evidence to create a picture of women in ancient Israel that differs from the biblical descriptions.

Stager, L.E. 1985. The Archaeology of the Family in Ancient Israel. *Bulletin of the American Schools of Oriental Research* 260: 1–35. A classic study of the ancient Israelite family that uses ethnographic and archaeological sources.

Notes

1 See Meyers 2005, 41–42 for the apotropaic (protective) use of light in the Hebrew Bible.
2 "Adah" is Hebrew for "ornament," another name that may have been chosen for its protective qualities (see Chapter 5).
3 See further Faust 2006 and Meyers 2002c for different views on egalitarianism in ancient Israel.
4 We should imagine an area overgrown with bushes and not a heavily wooded area, however (Callaway 1984, 58–60).
5 Graham-Brown 1980, chapter 1, photo 24.
6 See MacDonald 2008, chapter 10 and references therein.

Chapter 2

Childhood

Orah's Story

Orah loved *shevuot* more than any of the other holidays celebrated by her village. Like everyone, she was excited by the changing landscape as the weather became warmer and the wildflowers bloomed on the terraces and valleys surrounding her village. Since the wheat harvest was just about over and her labor was no longer needed in the fields, Orah was occasionally permitted to accompany her older male cousins to the pasture with the family's herd, and she loved these opportunities to escape the confines of the small village and run freely with the animals. While her cousins paid attention to the herd, Orah usually walked well behind with her spindle in hand, spinning thread out of the bunches of wool her father had shorn from the sheep just a few weeks earlier. Although her thread was still fairly rough and bumpy, she hoped to soon be able to make thread as smooth as that spun by her sister Adah. At eight years old, Orah had already been spinning wool for several years, and she usually carried bunches of wool and a spindle in a woven pouch to practice whenever she could.

What Orah liked most about the season, however, was helping her mother bake the wheat and barley bread that would be offered to Yahweh during the *shevuot* feast. It was a treat to bake these special loaves, which were made with freshly ground wheat and leavened with froth from the beer Orah helped her aunt brew from the barley harvested just weeks before. Although Orah could only grind grain for a short time, since she soon tired of moving the heavy upper stone across the lower grinding slab, she stayed close to her mother, sister and aunt as they ground on their sets of grinding stones in the courtyard, and helped them by collecting the flour into a bowl using a brush and piece of cloth. After enough grain had been ground, Orah and the women mixed the flour with water and leaven on pieces of cloth to form the loaves that would be baked later that day. When it was time, Orah was allowed to place some of the loaves on the layer of stones at the bottom of the dome-shaped oven in the corner of the courtyard. Orah, Adah and their mother huddled around the oven and offered prayers of thanks to Yahweh for the grain; while she prayed, Orah watched, fascinated, as the bread loaves baked in the small, hot oven, fueled by cakes of dung and small sticks that she had helped collect.

Although her entire family was exhausted from working in the fields and at the threshing floor by the end of the harvest season, they still found strength to make special preparations to thank Yahweh for the wheat harvest. In addition to preparing bread and other special food, Orah helped her father's concubine make several large jars to store some of the newly harvested grain as well as some shallow bowls that would be used during the feast itself. Orah enjoyed kneading the clay that her father and uncle brought up from the clay bed by the spring below the village, and rolling some of the long clay coils that the concubine would use to make the large pottery vessels. Although the concubine preferred to make and decorate the fine small bowls by herself, she sometimes allowed Orah to try her hand at painting simple, black geometric designs on some of the vessels; the concubine alone painted the intricate designs of birds and other animals in red and black paint, however. The women in Orah's house made pottery in the courtyard, and Orah helped the concubine place the vessels in a sheltered area by an outer wall to dry before they would be fired in a small bonfire in the days before the feast.

While the concubine made new jars and bowls, Orah's mother and Adah spent as much time as they could spare at the loom, weaving a new rug to replace one of the rugs in the main room that had too many holes in it to be of much use in this busy area. Orah's mother had dyed some of the woolen threads red using dried pomegranate rinds and black from burnt bone, and these threads would be woven to form patterns in the otherwise cream-colored cloth. The loom, which was made of two upright wooden poles set into small stone sockets, could be easily moved around the house, and the women often wove in the courtyard during this pleasant time of year. Orah sometimes helped her mother and sister with the weaving, but she was still quite slow at it; she could better contribute by practicing her spinning and performing other chores around the house, like tending the small garden in the courtyard and carrying water in a small jar up from the spring below the village.

During all of these activities, Orah's mother and aunt told stories about holidays past and taught Orah and the other children about the gods and goddesses worshiped by the household. Orah had already learned a number of songs about the gods, and she sang along with the women while they went about the monotonous and repetitive work of grinding grain and brewing beer, making pottery and weaving on the loom. When *shevuot* finally arrived, Orah's mother and father would recount the old stories to the rest of the family, and all would sing and say prayers of thanks to Yahweh for a successful harvest year. Orah was thrilled to be the one to place the loaves of bread baked from fresh grain on the mudbrick bench inside the entrance to the main room of the house as gifts to Yahweh for the harvest. Along with the rest of the village, Orah's family prayed for a successful grape harvest in the coming months and asked the gods to preserve the health of all of the people in the village. Orah's household enjoyed the feast of bread, beer, vegetables and boiled meat from the goat killed by Orah's father for this special occasion, and their spirits were revived as they prepared for the hot summer to come.

Introduction

Children were considered Yahweh's greatest gift in ancient Israel (Grassi 1992, 904). The first commandment found in Genesis (Gen. 1.28) is to have children, and successful conception, pregnancy, childbirth and infancy was a major focus of nearly every woman's life. The divine gift of children to barren women and elderly parents is the theme of several stories in Genesis. Childhood, now as then, is the formative period in a person's life; for a young girl in ancient Israel, it was the period during which she learned what she needed to know to prepare her for her future roles of wife and mother. In the central highland villages of the early Iron Age, all children were valued for the contributions that they could make to the economic success of their parents' households (Meyers 1998, 25), but the biblical writers do not offer much information about the specific activities, duties and expectations of a young girl. We are not even told of any initiation rites that would have accompanied an Israelite girl's entrance into puberty, except, perhaps, for the mourning period described in the story of Jephthah's daughter in Judg. 11.34-40. In Chapter 3, when Orah is 12 years old, we will witness some of the ritual activities that could have accompanied a girl's first menstruation.

The actual period of childhood in ancient Israel is hard to define because different cultures see this social category differently (Baxter 2005, 79). Contrary to our Western view that childhood is biologically defined, there is great variation in the way that societies define childhood, especially since many cultures do not emphasize chronological age but, rather, maturity (Kamp 2001, 3–4). Such was the case in early twentieth-century Palestine: an adult does not reckon a child's ages in years — or necessarily know his or her own exact age for that matter — because a person's approximate age is apparent from physical changes and the work that he or she can perform

(Granqvist 1931, 35). The activities of childhood described in this chapter are ones that would have occupied at least some of the time of a young Israelite girl between the ages of four and 12; Orah is eight years old in this chapter, the hypothetical midpoint between weaning (Chapter 6) and first menstruation (Chapter 3).

Scholars investigating the archaeology of children recently have made great strides in developing methodologies for making visible the supposedly invisible presence of children in the past; like women, children are often believed to be associated with private space rather than public space, which accounts for their perceived invisibility (Kamp 2001, 3). Some archaeologists have searched for evidence of children's acquisition of craft techniques, which has involved examining artifacts like pottery vessels for evidence of inexpert workmanship (Kamp 2001, 13), in an effort to find children and their contributions in the archaeological record. The biblical writers mention a few of the productive activities of young women and girls in the house and in the larger community: watering animals is apparently a task of young women (Gen. 29.7-8; Exod. 2.16), as is gleaning (Ruth 2.8) and participating in the cult of the queen of heaven by gathering wood in preparation for the baking of cakes (Jer. 7.18). But these few references do not offer much insight into the variety of a young girl's economic contributions to the early Iron Age household.

The ethnographic sources from Palestine are instructive, for they reveal that girls are responsible for many tasks from a young age. The very young girl "...hands things and chases the animals; she drives the chickens away from their sitting-place" (Granqvist 1931, 137). Children carried water, looked after goats, sheep and poultry, and helped at harvest time by threshing, winnowing, picking fruit and olives and gleaning.[1] Older girls were responsible for watching children (Grant 1907, 68). Reflecting on their own childhoods, Palestinian women talked about the things they could not do until they were about seven years old, which included combing their hair and baking (as they were too small before then to lean over the oven) (Granqvist 1931, 138). According to these women, the older girl is called a goatherd, a guardian of fig-trees, a woodgatherer and drawer of water (Granqvist 1931, 138).[2]

The main technologies discussed in this chapter — bread production, pottery making, spinning and weaving — are among the tasks most closely associated with females in traditional societies the world over according to a study that examined 185 societies documented in the HRAF (Human Relations Area Files) materials (Murdock and Provost 1973, table 1). On a scale of 1 to 50, with 1 being the activity most closely associated with men and 50 the activity most closely associated with women, preparing vegetal foods was ranked 50, cooking 49, pottery making 43, spinning 46 and weaving on a loom 38. Although these activities are sometimes carried out by men, the rankings show that these particular tasks are universally associated with women. Along with educating young children generally, these were among women's most important contributions to the village household in the Iron Age I, and thus the productive tasks that were most important for a girl to learn at an early age.

Education and Literacy

According to the Hebrew Bible, the education of young children was largely the responsibility of women (1 Sam. 1.22-28; Prov. 31.1), although both parents provided instruction to young girls and boys (Prov. 1.8). Parental education essentially included instruction in all of the essential activities that girls and boys would need to learn to be successful during their lifetimes. Although schools may have existed from the time of the United Monarchy, it is unlikely that there were organized schools in the central highlands during the early Iron Age. More important than literacy — which is the ability to read and write with some degree of fluency — was education in the tasks and responsibilities that were required for the success of the household. In addition to learning specific tasks, the day-to-day interactions between mothers and their children allowed for the transmission of aspects of Israelite culture (Meyers 1998, 256), since "during the enculturation process, children learn values as well as skills" (Kamp 2001, 14). Children learned about religious traditions, for example, by practicing them at home (see Chapter 3) and by accompanying their parents on pilgrimages to local shrines (Chapter 6).

The subject of literacy in early Iron Age Israel is not completely understood. Judges 8.14 indicates that Gideon learned to write early, but this does not necessarily mean that all children — or even all male children, since females rarely attended school in the ancient Near East — could read and write. Several inscriptions, including an inscribed jar handle from Khirbet Raddana and an abecedary (an inscription of the alphabet) from Izbet Sartah, were uncovered in Iron Age I contexts in these central highland villages; this attests to some level of literacy among the early Israelite population. The Gezer Calendar (see Chapter 1), an agricultural calendar that some believe may have been a schoolboy's exercise, is dated slightly later, to the second half of the tenth century BCE. The increasing number of inscribed artifacts from the ninth century seems to suggest that schools existed in Jerusalem and in the capitals of the northern kingdom of Israel during the remaining period of the monarchy (Lemaire 1992, 308–9).

Very young girls and boys were primarily under the care of their mothers and close female relatives until boys were old enough to work in the fields and perhaps learn the specialized crafts — like metalworking — practiced by their fathers. Although the public/private dichotomy of men leading lives outside of the home and women being restricted to the home was not the reality in the Iron Age I, it is likely that women spent more time in the household than men performing the domestic tasks — like baking and weaving — discussed below. Although boys certainly assisted with this work, they were also expected to learn the agricultural practices of their fathers when they were old enough to provide the physical labor; around age 13, children would have been able to contribute a full adult workload (Meyers 1997, 27). A father's role in disciplining his son is mentioned by the biblical writers in several places (Deut. 8.5; Prov. 29.17), and it appears from these passages that men assumed the primary responsibility for the education of their sons by a certain age. Girls learned primarily from their mothers (as suggested, perhaps, by Ezek. 16.44: "Like mother, like daughter") until they were married; women, naturally, would have taught the young girls in the household the daily life tasks in which they were often engaged.

Baking and Brewing

Although Orah is quite young in this chapter, she is already a practiced baker who contributes eagerly to the baking of the loaves required for the celebration of *shevuot*. She has already been involved in the arduous process of grinding grain using her family's sets of grinding stones for several years, and although she is not strong enough to grind for as long as her older sister, mother and aunt, she is quite capable of kneading dough and baking the loaves of bread required daily as well as assisting in the production of beer. In Orah's household, grinding barley and wheat is the most time-consuming and labor-intensive daily activity performed by the women; ethnographic accounts report that a woman might spend up to five hours a day grinding enough grain for the entire family (Wilson 1906, 117) to eat in the form of bread, porridge and gruel nearly every day of the year.

Bread's importance in the ancient Israelite diet is suggested by the meaning of the Hebrew word *lehem*, which literally means "bread" but is also a term used for food generally. The biblical expression "to eat bread" (Gen. 31.54; 37.25), which meant to share a meal, also shows that bread comprised a large part of the diet. Although the biblical writers do not provide detailed accounts of bread making, some passages give us insight into the customs and contexts of baking. Males sometimes baked bread at home (Gen. 19.3; 40.1), but bread was most often made by women in domestic settings (Gen. 18.6; Lev. 26.26; 1 Sam. 28.24; 2 Sam. 13.8; 1 Kgs 17.12-13), including palaces (1 Sam. 8.13). Commercial bakeries were established in larger towns like Jerusalem before the Exile (Jer. 37.21), and priests were responsible for making bread for use in the Tabernacle (Lev. 24.5) and in the Jerusalem Temple (Ezek. 46.20, 23-24); women, however, were responsible for baking cakes for the queen of heaven (Jer. 44.19) as part of the worship of this deity (Chapter 3).

Research on bread making in ancient Egypt demonstrates that transforming cereal grains into food and drink was a complicated process that required the use of a number of specialized tools and installations, many of which do not survive in the archaeological record of Syro-Palestine. In Egypt, there is archaeological evidence for the use of numerous tools in the bread-making process, including sieves, winnowing baskets, trays, paddles, stone mortars, wooden pestles, handstones, querns, brushes, jars and pieces of cloth for collecting flour from around grinding areas (Samuel 1999, 122). Due to the bias of preservation, the archaeological remains of bread production in ancient Israel are usually limited to ground stone tools and several types of cooking installation, although surely many of the tools made of perishable materials known from ancient Egypt were used in Israel as well.

The process of making bread in ancient Israel required a number of steps. After cereals — most commonly barley and wheat — were harvested in spring, they were threshed on a threshing floor to separate the grain from the stalks and other inedible parts of the plant. After threshing, the remaining material was tossed into the air using large winnowing forks so the wind could further separate the material and then further refined using woven sieves and baskets to remove more of the inedible particles. It was then poured into woven sacks made of goats' hair or wool and carried back to the household. Grain was stored in plastered or stone-lined storage pits dug into house floors, although it could also be stored in ceramic vessels (1 Kgs 17.12) or mud-plastered bins. Grain must have been carefully rationed and protected from pests to ensure there would be enough for the entire year.

When it was time to bake bread, grain might be pounded in a mortar using a pestle (both could be made of stone or wood), either wet or dry, before it was ground into flour using grinding stones (also called handstones, grinding slabs and querns). Grinding was accomplished by moving a relatively small handstone back and forth with both hands across the grains on a larger, heavier grinding slab or quern until they were reduced to flour, which was then collected and either temporarily stored or used immediately to make bread. Handstones and grinding slabs/querns were made of the dark volcanic stone called basalt if it was available, because basalt has self-sharpening qualities that make grinding more efficient and produces less grit than other types of stone (Ebeling and Rowan 2004).

Although heavy, grinding slabs are portable and were probably operated either indoors or outdoors according to the weather or season; indeed, grinding stones are found in various parts of Iron Age houses and courtyards, showing that grinding could be performed just about anywhere. According to ethnographic sources from Palestine, grinding was often done in the courtyard,[3] although the small stone handmills used a century ago would have been moved indoors or to another sheltered location in bad weather. Groups of women in ancient Israelite villages may have sat together grinding grain and sharing information; this would have been an important time for education and instruction, as well as gossiping and storytelling, since women were occupied for up to several hours a day in this monotonous activity (Meyers 2002a).

Freshly-ground flour was likely used up quickly, as it did not keep for long. To make bread, one could simply knead flour with water and a bit of salt — if it was available — in a bowl, trough, on a large stone or on a piece of cloth. According to the Hebrew Bible, this unleavened bread was prepared when baking was done in haste (Exod. 12.39), when ritual demanded it (Exod. 13.6-7; Lev. 2.5; 23.6) and on other occasions (Gen. 19.3). If lighter, tastier leavened bread was desired, yeast could be added from a leftover piece of bread, grape skins or beer froth, or one could wait for airborne organisms to leaven the kneaded dough. Leavened bread and cakes made in various shapes and baked with additives like oil, honey, date syrup, herbs and spices were apparently common in ancient Israel judging from the many biblical references to them.

According to biblical descriptions, bread could be baked in an oven (Lev. 2.4), on a ceramic or iron griddle set upon stones over a fire pit or hearth (Lev. 2.5; 7.9) or directly on a hot stone in ashes (1 Kgs 19.6). There are many archaeological examples of ovens and hearths from Iron Age sites; generally they are found inside houses, although they are also found in exterior courtyards, streets, open areas, paved areas and in public buildings (Baadsgaard 2008, 28). Two types of beehive-shaped ovens are known from archaeological excavations: the *tabun* (an Arabic term) and the biblical *tannur*. The *tabun* features a flat interior surface often lined with stones on which bread was placed for baking. Fuel would have been piled up against the outer surface of the oven to heat the interior. The *tannur* was a similarly shaped oven, but it differed from the *tabun* in that a fire was set inside the bottom of the oven and dough was slapped on the hot interior walls for baking (Baadsgaard 2008, 21). These flat loaves baked quickly and were peeled off to cool outside the oven. Pieces of wood, cakes of animal dung mixed with straw and the leftovers from olive pressing were used as fuel.

Ovens that are found outside of houses in open or public spaces tend to be larger than those found inside houses, which suggests that they were shared by several households or the larger community. Larger ovens were also built in courtyards and other exterior spaces for cooking during the hot summer months and probably for smoke dispersal. The association of other food processing equipment with ovens reveals patterns of household bread baking, and the close proximity of tools related to other domestic activities, like weaving, may evidence spaces where women worked on various household tasks in groups (Baadsgaard 2008). The ethnographic evidence from Palestine shows that women from several neighboring families might share a communal oven. A woman might spend hours around the oven waiting for her turn to bake, all the while catching up with the neighborhood women while also doing needlework, sewing or embroidery (Grant 1907, 78–79; Wilson 1906, 120–21).

There is very little art from ancient Israel that illustrates bread production. A clay figurine from the Phoenician site of Akhviz (Figure 2.1), on the northern coast of modern Israel, depicts a figure (probably a woman) kneading bread in a trough. There are many statues, paintings and models from ancient Egypt, however, that illustrate various stages in the bread-making process. From these images we learn a number of things about the technology and context of bread production, and in the vast majority of bread-making scenes it is women who are shown grinding grain, kneading dough and baking bread (Curtis 2001, 112, 115–16, 127, figures 8–9).

Although bread was a staple in ancient Israel, grain could be consumed in other ways: it could be eaten raw, soaked in water and consumed as porridge or gruel, parched or fermented to make beer. Brewing was an offshoot of bread production in the ancient Near East and Egypt because beer was usually made from bread that was crumbled and added to a jar of water; Eccl. 11.1-2 may refer to throwing bread in water to make beer (Homan 2002). Yeast was then intentionally added to the liquid mixture or yeast spores in the air would ferment the liquid, and after a few days the beer was ready to drink either plain or flavored with fruits and spices. Beer does not store well and it was thus made for immediate consumption; unlike wine (Chapter 3), which could only be made during the summer grape harvest, beer could be made anytime during the year from stored grains. Fermenting grains increases calories and adds protein and other vitamins, and the small amount of alcohol

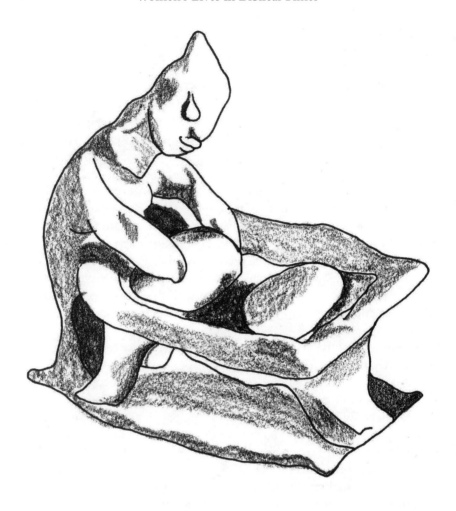

2.1 Kneading trough (after Vamosh 2007, 13).

in this homemade beer would have killed off bacteria present in the water, making beer more nutritious and generally safer to drink than water. Women are most closely associated with beer production at the household level in the ancient Near East and Egypt, and we can imagine that women produced beer in ancient Israel as well (Ebeling and Homan 2008).

The biblical term *shekar*, usually translated as "strong drink," is best translated as "beer," or possibly a beverage made of grain and fruits (Homan 2004). According to the biblical writers, beer was to be drunk at sacrificial meals (Deut. 14.26) and was required for Temple ritual (Num. 28.7–10). Hannah, who was accused by the priest Eli of being drunk at the Tabernacle in Shiloh (1 Sam. 1.12-15), said that she drank neither wine nor *shekar*, showing that *shekar* was a different alcoholic beverage from wine. Women and men who wanted to become a Nazirite — or consecrated person — were required to give up wine and *shekar* (Num 6.1-4).

As discussed above, ethnographic sources demonstrate that, in traditional societies, women are strongly associated with baking bread and cooking; coupled with the biblical, iconographic and archaeological evidence, we can imagine that the same was true in ancient Israel. We still know relatively little about household brewing in ancient Israel, but given the technology required for producing beer and the relative preciousness of wine, it is likely that women brewed beer for household consumption as well. In Orah's household, all of the adult women made bread daily, and Orah watched and assisted the women in order to learn how to perform this vital task, which was required for the celebration of *shevuot* and other important occasions (see Chapter 3). Baking bread — along with brewing beer — may have been the single most important daily-life activity that Orah would need to learn to prepare for her future role as head of her husband's household.

Pottery Production

Ceramic vessels, which were invented in the ancient Near East during the Neolithic Period (c. 6000 BCE), are ubiquitous at Iron Age sites and constitute the artifact category best understood by archaeologists. We know more about ancient Israelite pottery than we do about any other craft or household technology, although archaeologists have primarily used pottery as a tool for establishing chronology — since pottery forms change gradually over time and a sequence is well established for ancient Israel — rather than a means of investigating women's technological contributions. Pottery vessels were used extensively in daily-life activities like storing, cooking, preparing and serving foods, and are found in abundance in more specialized locations, like temples and tombs, as well.

As mentioned above, women are the primary potters in traditional societies and it is likely that women were responsible for creating the handmade, undecorated pottery intended for household use in ancient Israel. Ethnographic evidence suggests that pot making is often passed down through the female line, and women take their potting skills and designs with them when they move to their husband's households in patrilineal societies; in twentieth-century Palestine, women learned the craft from their mothers and grandmothers (Amiry and Tamari 1989, 43). In our story, Orah learns how to make ceramic vessels by watching and helping all of the adult women in her household, but she is especially interested in learning from her father's concubine, who comes to Orah's village with special potting skills and a different ceramic tradition.

Pottery vessels that are fired in a kiln do not break down easily; unlike food remains, textiles and other organic materials, ceramics preserve very well in the climate of Israel. However, we must keep in mind that innumerable containers made of perishable materials like woven bags (see below), baskets (see Chapter 5) and animal skins (see Chapter 6) must have been important in ancient Israel as well, even if they do not tend to survive in archaeological contexts. Luckily, we know quite a bit about the pottery traditions in ancient Israel from their actual remains, since the biblical writers provide very little specific information about pottery production and technology. The image of the potter is sometimes used metaphorically, as when Yahweh is portrayed as a potter and creator of humans out of earth (Gen. 2.7; 19; Isa. 64.8), and male potters are mentioned in several passages (1 Chron. 4.23; Jer. 18.2-4), but these refer to the industrial production of ceramic vessels outside of the home during the period of the monarchy. There are no references at all to women making pottery for household use in the Hebrew Bible.

The pottery-making process involved the following general steps: digging and preparing the clay, forming the vessels, decorating, drying and firing. Most of these steps can be carried out in or near the potter's house, and ethnographic accounts show that all family members, including children, contribute to the process (Matson 2001, 1555). The only clear archaeological evidence for pottery production in the domestic context is the rare discovery of pottery kilns and stone potters' wheels; otherwise, the manufacture of ceramic vessels leaves behind traces that are often missed by archaeologists. This is probably because pottery-making sites are seasonal and ceramic vessels are produced in the same household spaces used for myriad other activities. Gloria London, who has conducted ceramic ethnoarchaeological fieldwork in Cyprus and the Philippines, describes how difficult it can be to identify domestic pottery production areas: "off-season, winter visits cause most observers to conclude that no pottery was or would ever be made in those same spaces. The complete absence of pottery, clay, or tools is due to the multi-functional use of space, depending on the season" (London 2008, 179).

We can imagine that mixing clay and forming, decorating and drying vessels were accomplished in the courtyard and inside the house during the dry season. According to Palestinian ethnography, the potting season began in spring, after the rainy season, when vessels could be dried before firing and there were enough tree branches available to collect for the firing pit. Young women in the family helped skilled — and presumably older — women dig and prepare the clay, while the skilled potters alone formed the vessels. Ethnographic research conducted in various parts of the world has shown that primary forming and shaping techniques require skills and knowledge passed down from generation to generation, and there is less evidence for experimentation in these initial stages than is seen in secondary finishing work and surface treatment (London 2008, 164). In Palestine, pots were left to dry in the courtyard for several weeks and were then fired in a pit or bread oven in the courtyard while women sang songs to prevent the pots from breaking (Amiry and Tamari 1989, 44). According to one source, women were seen making huge, hand-built water jars that were then fired by heaping dung around them and setting fire to the pile (Wilson 1906, 251).

The typical pottery of the Iron Age I villages is utilitarian, evidence that the pottery was made by local residents for their own use (Bloch-Smith and Nakhai 1999, 76). The fact that nearly all the pottery is undecorated may support its utilitarian function. According to the ethnographic sources, pottery vessels were handmade by women in Palestine;[4] the potter's wheel was used only in the towns, where men produced a different sort of functional, and decorated, pottery for the market (Amiry and Tamari 1989, 43). Decorated pottery is known in Iron Age I Israel, but it is found primarily along the Mediterranean coast and is characteristic of Philistine ceramic traditions; Philistine bichrome pottery, which features geometric designs as well as bird and animal motifs in red and black paint, has been identified at only four sites in the central highlands during this period (Faust 2006, 211). The decorated pottery that Orah's father's concubine makes for *shevuot* is thus atypical and foreign to the villagers.

The types of pottery found in Iron Age I villages include vessels used primarily for storing, cooking and serving foods, and there is considerable overlap in the functions of different vessel types. Large, closed vessels like collar rim storage jars were used primarily for storing water, although other liquids, grain, flour and preserved foods like dried fruits and fish could be stored in them as well. Archaeological remains of large jars are found in various parts of the lower floors of Iron Age houses; ethnographic accounts indicate that they were propped against walls or in corners and used to store water, olive oil and olives (Grant 1907, 76). Widemouth vessels like cooking pots were used for cooking foods over a hearth, since their large openings would allow for stirring; a flat stone or pottery sherd could be placed over the opening of the vessel to retain heat. Large bowls (kraters) could be used for mixing and serving foods and small open bowls may have been used for individual drinking and eating. The only utensil available was the knife, so food was either eaten with the hands or sopped up with bread (Borowski 2003, 73–74).

Ceramic vessels were essential for many daily-life activities in the ancient Israelite house, and vessels for household use were most likely made by adult women assisted by various family members. Women might have achieved higher status and value in their families as a result of their potting skills; the ethnographic sources relate that a skilled potter fetched a higher bride price than a woman of average skill in Palestine a century ago (Wilson 1906, 109–10). Orah's participation in pot making as a young girl both helped the adult women in the house and prepared Orah to make utilitarian pottery in the future for her own use. After she is married, Orah will take the ceramic traditions of her childhood to her husband's house, and thus carry on the traditions of her own village and family — including those of her husband's concubine — by teaching them to her future daughter and the other young women in her husband's household.

Spinning and Weaving

In this story, Orah's sister Adah has already proved to be a gifted spinner and weaver. Orah is still mastering the spinning required to make woolen thread, although she has been practicing already for several years. Like baking and producing pottery, spinning and weaving were primarily female activities in antiquity, and producing thread and cloth were among the most important ways a woman could contribute to the household economy. A variety of important items for personal use and for use in and around the household were woven, including clothing (see Chapter 5), rugs, bedding and blankets, curtains, containers, tents, wall hangings and much more. Palestinian women in the early twentieth century still made household items like rugs, storage bags, saddle bags and hammock cradles for carrying babies at home even when fabric for clothing could be purchased.[5]

There are several biblical references to spinning and weaving, and all describe the work of women. Women in the Exodus spun materials for the Tabernacle: "All the skillful women spun with their hands, and brought what they had spun in blue and purple and crimson yarns and fine linen; all the women whose hearts moved them to use their skill spun the goats' hair" (Exod. 35.25-26). In another sacred context — the Jerusalem Temple — women wove garments for the image of the goddess Asherah (2 Kgs 23.7). The woman of valor in Proverbs 31 is both a spinner and a weaver; in fact, the largest number of specific tasks mentioned in this passage concerns making wool and linen cloth (Ackerman 2008, 15–16).

Spinning is a relatively simple process that nevertheless takes practice to perfect. Wool was the principal fiber that was available for spinning in ancient Israel, although other fibers, including flax and goats' hair, were spun as well. Flax may have been cultivated in the Iron Age I period, but direct evidence for this is lacking; growing flax is more closely associated with Egypt in the biblical text (Exod. 9.31; Isa. 19.9). Flax is mentioned by the biblical writers as a material used in weaving (Deut. 22.11, Prov. 31.13) and, in Josh. 2.6, Rahab hides the Israelite spies sent by Joshua among stalks of flax that were drying on her roof. Linen garments made from the flax plant (see Chapter 4) would have been expensive in ancient Israel, and thus worn primarily by the wealthy and elite (King and Stager 2001, 150).

Processing flax for spinning requires retting, which is essentially soaking the stalks in water to separate the usable fibers; in contrast, wool only has to be washed after shearing in order to spin it. To produce woolen thread, the fibers could simply be rubbed or rolled on the upper leg or another flat surface. Much more efficient spinning was accomplished by carefully drawing the fibers with one hand onto a spindle — a rod made out of a stick or length of bone — with an attached spindle whorl. The whorl was literally a weight attached to the bottom of the spindle that kept it spinning; in antiquity it was most often made of clay, such as a reworked pot sherd, but a rock could be used or even a piece of fruit or vegetable (Barber 1994, 37–38). The spun thread was then wrapped around the spindle before it could unwind. Spinning thread required tools that could be made rather easily and cheaply, and it was an activity that could be carried out anytime, while walking, sitting or even doing other tasks. The archaeological remains of spinning from Iron Age Israel consist mainly of spindle whorls, which were often made of inorganic materials like clay; wooden spindles and the fibers and threads themselves only rarely survive.

Weaving is a much more complicated technology that involves interlacing two sets of threads — the warp threads and the weft threads — at right angles to each other (Barber 1994, 39). The warp must be held under tension to allow for the weft fibers to be passed through them to create a weave; the loom is the device used to apply tension to the warp threads. Two types of loom invented in Anatolia in the Neolithic Period were used in early Israel: the horizontal ground loom and a vertical warp-weighted loom. Archaeological evidence for the warp-weighted loom is easier to detect because loom weights made of clay, stone or other materials were required to hold the warp thread under tension. Wooden loom fragments survive less often, but caches of loom weights indicate the presence of one or more looms, and the actual weight of the individual loom weights helps specialists identify the production of either light or heavy weaves (Friend 1998, 8–10).

The horizontal ground loom is harder to detect because it was simply a wooden frame staked to the ground. Most of our evidence for this type of loom comes from artistic depictions from ancient Egypt, and the weavers in these scenes are always women. Paintings and detailed three-dimensional wooden models of weaving workshops like one from the Middle Kingdom (c. 2055–1650 BCE) tomb of Meketre show weavers working together on horizontal looms staked to the ground, while women process the flax, spin and measure warp threads nearby (Barber 1994, 80–81). Since organic material preserves in the Egyptian climate, there are numerous archaeological examples from ancient Egypt of clothing items, household objects like bedding and bags, and textiles used in industry, agriculture, medicine, religion and funerary contexts; these finds suggest the widespread use of textiles in ancient Israel as well (Vogelsang-Eastwood 2000, 286–96).

Since wool was the fiber most readily available for spinning in the central highlands, spinning could be carried out anytime after the spring shearing and until the supply of wool ran out. According to one ethnographic source, the weaving season began in spring and lasted until September or October — or as long as the weather remained dry — since weaving was done mainly in the courtyard (Amiry and Tamari 1989, 46). Archaeological remains of spindle whorls and the clay weights used to operate warp-weighted looms are found in various contexts within Iron Age houses, demonstrating that spinning and weaving could be carried out in different parts of the household; as with grinding stones, the portable warp-weighted loom could be moved from room to room or to the courtyard depending on the weather conditions.

Because of the poor preservation of organic material in this region, not many textile fragments from the Iron Age survive. The more than 100 textile fragments from the desert site of Kuntillat 'Ajrud, which dates to the ninth–eighth centuries BCE, are an unusual find, and the preponderance of linen in the assemblage (only 11 pieces were wool) and mixed cloth of wool and flax may indicate that this rare material was required for use in cultic activities at the site (Sheffer and Tidhar 1991, 14).[6] Loom weights and the remains of wool threads comprise other archaeological evidence for weaving activities at Kuntillat 'Ajrud, although it is unclear if the spinners and weavers at this specialized site were women.

As with most other village crafts in early twentieth-century Palestine, weaving was the responsibility of women, and the men's share in the production was the shearing of the animals and the marketing of the women's textiles in nearby towns and villages. According to one observer, "[t]he weaving was done on a horizontal ground loom, the treadle loom being used only by town craftsmen. It was customary to see many looms neatly stretched out on the ground, with groups of two or three women sitting weaving at one end of the loom, while onlookers sat around exchanging news and creating an atmosphere of merriment to relieve the monotony of the weavers' work" (Amiry and Tamari 1989, 47). It is possible that women worked in groups on one or more looms in ancient Israel; as in women's grinding groups, this would have been an important time for the transmission of news and information among women in the household and village, as well as the opportunity to share knowledge related to this important craft (Meyers 2003a, 435–36).

In our story, Orah spins thread when she accompanies her cousins to the pasture with the flocks and spins at home at other times as well. Although she is not yet able to weave textiles by herself, she assists her mother and sister on the loom when they need her help. Since it took many hours of work to make even a simple garment, Orah's help was required to perform the seemingly never-ending task of spinning thread and weaving in the household. From all of the available evidence, we can conclude that spinning and weaving — along with cooking and making pottery — were the quintessential "women's work" in antiquity, including in ancient Israel. In the largely self-sufficient Iron Age I village, girls' and women's contributions were critical, and passing down these crafts, technologies and customs were the most important ways that adult women educated their female children.

For Further Reading

Barber, E. W. 1994. *Women's Work: The First 20,000 Years. Women, Cloth, and Society in Early Times*. New York: W. W. Norton and Company. A thorough discussion of the early development of spinning and weaving technology in the ancient world. Barber masterfully uses the evidence to describe spinning and weaving as women's arts from prehistory until the Industrial Revolution.

Curtis, R. I. 2001. *Ancient Food Technology*. Leiden: Brill. A comprehensive study of the development of food technology in the ancient Near East, Egypt and Mediterranean world from prehistory through the Roman Empire. It is particularly useful for its discussion of the political and economic roles food technology played in these ancient societies.

London, G.A. 2008. Fe(male) Potters as the Personifications of Individuals, Places, and Things as Known from Ethnoarchaeological Studies. In *Women in the Ancient and Classical Near East*, ed. B.A. Nakhai, 155–80. Newcastle upon Tyne: Cambridge Scholars Press. This study uses ethnoarchaeological fieldwork conducted by the author in Cyprus and the Philippines to inform on the process of pottery production, reasons for the absence of evidence for pottery production in archaeological contexts and the roles of women in pottery manufacture.

Nicholson, P.T. and I. Shaw, eds. 2000. *Ancient Egyptian Materials and Technology*. 2000. Cambridge University Press. Includes a number of studies by specialists in ancient Egyptian technologies that are useful for understanding similar phenomena in ancient Israel. A number of the individual studies are cited in the remaining chapters of this book.

Notes

1 Graham-Brown 1980, 42; chapter 1, photos 10–11, 14–15 and 24–25; Grant 1907, photo, p. 132.

2 A description of a day in the life of a girl in the village of Artas nearly a century ago is particularly illuminating, as it shows that the work of a growing girl is an adult woman's work in miniature. The girl described was about nine years old; she is called "attendant on her mother." She brings utensils to her mother while her mother is cooking, brings mattresses and cushions and opens and shuts the door. She carries her brother and puts him to sleep in his cradle, airs the bedclothes and sweeps. If her mother is out, she plays with her little brother. She helps prepare the oven for baking by gathering stones and fuel for the fire (Granqvist 1931, 138–39). All of this work is seen as a very important part of a girl's education, and Palestinian women say that mothers teach their daughters while fathers teach their sons.

3 Amiry and Tamari 1989, 17–20; Graham-Brown 1980, chapter 1, photo 41.

4 Graham-Brown 1980, chapter 1, photos 53–54; London and Sinclair 1991.

5 Amiry and Tamari 1989, 48; Graham-Brown 1980, chapter 1, photo 23.

6 Mixing wool and linen fibers is forbidden according to Lev. 19.19 and Deut. 22.11, but mandated for priestly garments that were embroidered with woolen thread of different colors (Exod. 28.6).

Chapter 3
Womanhood

It was an exciting but melancholy time in Orah's household the summer of her twelfth year. Her parents were making arrangements for her sister Adah's marriage, and soon Adah would leave her birth house and move to her new husband's house in a village a few hours' walk away. Their mother was visibly anxious for Adah's upcoming wedding celebrations and she kept everyone busy with its preparations, especially pressing grapes to make wine from the first harvest. Although she was kept busy and distracted from dawn until dusk, Orah found time to be depressed that her sister would be leaving so soon. Perhaps because of her sadness, Orah felt a little bit sick, and she complained to her sister that it would only get worse when Adah left. Although Adah's mind was understandably elsewhere these days, she took notice of Orah's complaints, observed once again how much she had matured and knew that her time could come any day now. Adah told Orah that she would not be surprised if Orah knew the way of women even before the wedding, but Orah only scoffed; her mother and sister had been telling her for years what it would be like when her first blood appeared, and she thought it would never actually happen to her.

But Adah was right. A few days later, Orah noticed spots of blood on her undergarments when she went to relieve herself in the stand of trees outside the village while doing the morning chores. Excitedly, she ran back to the house and reported what had happened to Adah and their mother, both of whom were weaving a cloth for Adah's wedding on the loom in the courtyard. Adah and their mother quickly abandoned the loom and accompanied Orah to the west room on the first floor of the house. There, they located the supply of rags and old pieces of wool felt they kept for this occasion. Adah, her mother, her aunt and the concubine were all menstruating themselves, and there were only a few cloths left for Orah to use that day. They showed her how to put the material in her undergarments, and pointed out the vessel of water in a corner of the room where she was to put her used cloths to soak before they would be rinsed by one of the women the next morning. When they were no longer needed, the clean cloths would be wrapped and packed away in a basket in the west room for use a few weeks later.

Orah's mother reminded Orah that she would need to take care around the men of the house when they returned from the vineyard, as their tradition limited contact between men and menstruating women. That evening, her mother told her, Orah would bake the special cakes for the goddess Astarte and offer them to her in the cult corner in the west room. In the late afternoon, after Orah was allowed to enjoy a nap, Adah and her mother prepared the parched grain for the evening meal and set aside a bowl of wheat flour they had ground earlier. When the rest of the evening meal was nearly ready, but before the men and older children had returned, Orah was summoned to the cooking area in the main room of the house. Her mother gave her the bowl of flour, some olive oil and a handful of raisins, and all of the women in the house said a blessing to Astarte as Orah kneaded the dough and formed two small bread cakes in the rough shape of the goddess. She carefully placed them on the layer of hot stones at the bottom of the small oven as she had seen her mother and sister do before, but this time they were her own cakes, and Orah felt proud of her ability to finally participate in this important female ritual. A few minutes later, she carefully pulled the baked cakes out of the oven using old cloths and let them cool on a dish near the entrance to the west room.

Later that evening, the women gathered in the west room to eat their meal by lamplight while the men ate the food that the women had left for them in the cool breeze of the courtyard. After the meal, the men and young children quickly brushed off the dishes and returned them to the storage room next to the west room before retreating to the roof to sleep. Two of the men, one of them Orah's father, returned to the terraces to sleep in the shelter and guard the vineyard for the night. They were all aware that this was the women's time, and Orah's absence at the evening meal signaled to them that she was with the other women behind the curtain that separated the west room from the main room of the house.

The house was quite dark when Orah's aunt lit the ceramic incense burner that stood on a low mudbrick altar in the west room and Orah placed her dish of cooled cakes next to it. Three small clay figurines of the goddess leaned against the wall at the back of the bench, and a bowl of grapes from the recent harvest sat before them. Orah's mother threw some droplets of olive oil on Orah's cakes and Adah poured beer into a small bowl next to them. As the other women offered food, drink and incense to the goddess, they thanked her for giving them the ability to have children and asked for the protection of all women and children in the house. They all quietly sang the ancient song about the goddess as Orah's mother gently tapped the small hand drum kept on the floor next the altar. Orah's mother then produced two bronze anklets from a pouch tied on a belt around her waist and gave them to Orah; the anklets symbolized Orah's transformation from girl to young woman and marked her as marriageable in their community. The women spent what seemed like hours recounting their first menstruation experiences, telling stories about the goddess and discussing the preparations for Adah's wedding. Her mother told Orah that a jar of wine from this year's pressing would be stored specifically for Orah's future wedding. Orah felt at ease in the company of these women — the closest people in her life — and slept solidly on a mat on the floor until daybreak.

During the next few days Orah learned how to act during her woman's time, as there were specific customs that she had to keep while she was bleeding. Although her daily chores were basically the same as always, she had to be careful not to handle the men's clothing or bedding. Orah kept closer to home than usual, and she was secretly glad to have a few days' break from the messy job of grape pressing. Orah's mother gave her a small bottle of special perfume to wear during the days of her period, and Orah was careful to apply the sweet liquid pressed by one of the women in the village sparingly. At the end of the five days of Orah's bleeding, she and Adah walked to the spring outside of the village to bathe; although Adah told her to be quick as she looked out for passersby, Orah was delighted by the rare opportunity to wash herself completely and she splashed in the stream of water until Adah begged her to get out. Orah was distracted just enough by these new events and thoughts of her own future to not be so anxious about Adah's imminent departure.

Introduction

Twelve was about the age when the ancient Israelite girl transitioned from childhood to adulthood as she physically became a woman. Although little is known of the coming-of-age rituals and initiation rites practiced in ancient Israel, we can imagine that the onset of female and male adolescence was an important time for the individual and her or his family. For women, rituals involving one or more deities probably marked the transition from girlhood to womanhood and served to celebrate the young woman's new ability to conceive. Since bearing children was the ultimate goal of every woman in ancient Israel, and one of the few chances a woman had to achieve status in her family and community (see Chapter 5), first menstruation was considered a blessing. But blood was also considered dangerous in ancient Israel, and menstruation was a threat to ritual purity and had to be controlled.

In our story, Orah's first menstruation is marked with a gift of perfume from her mother, who has acquired this precious substance from a woman in the village who presses perfume from locally available plants. Orah's perfume and the incense burned by her aunt in the west room serve to mask odor and invoke the goddess Astarte during this special time. Orah is glad to be relieved of her wine-pressing duties for a few days, and she remains closer to home than usual until she is permitted to clean herself and return to her normal life along with Adah and the other women in her household.

Grape Harvest and Wine Making

Orah's coming-of-age takes place in late June, during the first grape harvest of the year. Early grapes ripen in Israel in June or July, and the vintage season occurs in August and September (King and Stager 2001, 99). The grape harvest was a time for celebration and feasting, and several biblical passages provide details of the shouting, dancing and singing that accompanied wine making. In Judg. 21.19-23, for example, the local girls dance near the vineyard at Shiloh, and Isa. 16.10 and Jer. 48.33 describe the joyous noises that accompanied the grape harvest (Walsh 2000, 181–83). Although beer, water and perhaps milk were common, everyday beverages in ancient Israel, wine was valued in Israelite society in part because it could only be made during the summer months; thus, wine was probably produced and stored for special occasions. In our story, one of the most important ways that Orah prepares for her sister Adah's upcoming wedding is by helping her family produce wine from the newly ripened grapes. We learn that some of this wine will be stored for Orah's future wedding as well.

The importance of wine in ancient Israel is demonstrated by the many biblical attestations to grapes and wine as well as wine's place in religious ritual and law codes (Borowski 2002, 103). In addition, there are nine terms for wine in the Hebrew Bible that comment either on different kinds, origins or characteristics (King and Stager 2001, 101). Although we can currently say little about the different types of wine made in the highlands in the Iron Age I period, archaeological evidence suggests the production of raisin wine: an eleventh-century BCE jug from Shiloh was found with its strainer next to a pile of raisins, which was interpreted as the residue from raisin wine strained and drunk at the site (Dayagi-Mendels 1999, 36). Raisins, fruitcakes and other preserved foodstuffs could also be made from grapes;

freshly squeezed grape juice, which must be consumed quickly before it starts to ferment from the naturally occurring yeast on grape skins, was probably not an important product.

Growing grapes — viticulture — was practiced in Palestine from at least the fourth millennium BCE, as attested by the seeds of cultivated grapes from the site of Tell esh-Shuna in the Jordan Valley (Dayagi-Mendels 1999, 15). The biblical writers seem to have been aware of the great antiquity of viticulture; this is evident in Gen. 9.20, which recounts that Noah's first act upon leaving the ark was to plant a vineyard (Borowski 2002, 102). Wine produced in Palestine was apparently exported to Egypt by one of the first pharaohs, the Dynasty 0 King Scorpion, who was buried at Abydos with some 700 wine jars (McGovern 2003, 91–103). Patrick McGovern analyzed the vessels and discovered that they were made in Palestine; he concluded that "they were used to collect wine produced in the same areas for storage and export" (McGovern 2003, 101).

Wine was very important in the economy of Canaan in the succeeding Middle and Late Bronze Ages, c. 2000–1200 BCE, and continued to be produced in the Iron Age. Grapes grew well in the thin hillside soil in the highlands of ancient Israel, and Orah's family worked some terraced plots just outside the village where grapes, olives, pomegranates and figs were cultivated. Although the book of Judges describes vineyards located at some distance from settlements (Judg. 14.5), archaeological excavations at Iron Age I sites have uncovered hillside agricultural terracing located just outside the highland villages. Grapes could only be harvested from vines that were at least four years old, so planting a vineyard was a sign of permanent settlement and investment in the land and its protection was critical. In this story, it is more likely that the grapes were guarded by men sleeping in temporary shelters (Isa. 1.8) than more costly stone watchtowers (Isa. 5.2).

Grapevines could be trained in a variety of ways, although it seems likely that, in the highlands, they were either allowed to spread along the warmth of the ground to bring an earlier crop (Dayagi-Mendels 1999, 18) or trained upward on trellises or poles so that grapes were more accessible to harvest, but out of reach of animals. For maximum yield, excessive branches had to be pruned regularly; this was accomplished in the fall with a pruning knife resembling a sickle (Borowski 2002, 107–9).

The technology of wine production can be reconstructed from representations of viticulture on wall paintings and reliefs in Egyptian tombs dating from the Old to New Kingdom. Biblical and other textual references also illuminate different stages in the wine making process. The New Kingdom (c. 1550–1069 BCE) tomb of Nakht in Thebes reveals various stages of wine production, including gathering clusters of grapes from vines, in this case trained on a pergola, and treading the harvested grapes on a winepress. Other details in the scene reveal that the juice flowed down from the press into a vat and ceramic jars were located nearby for wine storage. An Old Kingdom (c. 2649–2134 BCE) stone relief from a tomb in Saqqara shows musicians accompanying winetreaders (Dayagi-Mendels 1999, 21).

Grapes were harvested by cutting the clusters with a pruning knife and collecting them in baskets. The grapes were then carried to stone winepresses located either in the vineyard or in the settlement. In the Iron Age I, it seems that rock-cut pressing installations were constructed in the vineyards and not in the villages. The simplest winepress was in the form of two rock-cut oval or rectangular basins, one carved into the bedrock at a lower level than the other. The two basins were connected by a channel (Walsh 2000, 148–49). The upper basin was the treading platform, and as grapes were trod the juice flowed through the channel and into the lower basin, where it might be left to ferment (King and Stager 2001, 100). Otherwise, the fermenting wine could be scooped into jars or wineskins and brought back to the house to be poured into larger jars for further fermentation and storage (Walsh 2000, 190–92).

Fermenting wine releases carbon dioxide, and ceramic containers for fermenting wine must have some sort of vent or opening to permit the release of gases. Archaeological evidence of pierced clay balls used as stoppers on wine bottles has been identified at a number of sites. After the wine had fermented, mud, straw or some other substance would be placed in the perforation of the clay ball to seal the jar and ensure that it would not turn into vinegar (Walsh 2000, 192). Wine might be stored in this way for up to a year. When it was served, a juglet was used to dip wine out of a large storage jar. It could then be strained to separate out foreign matter; the archaeological remains of bronze strainers as part of drinking sets have been uncovered at Iron Age sites. It was then consumed from shallow bowls, as seen on iconographic representations from ancient Israel such as a thirteenth–twelfth century BCE ivory plaque from Megiddo that shows a ruler sitting on a throne and drinking wine out of a bowl. In this scene, two servants stand behind the ruler and draw wine from a larger vessel (Dayagi-Mendels 1999, 82). Ceramic jars, juglets and cups that could have been used for storing and drinking wine are found in quantity in Iron Age sites.

Harvesting grapes and producing wine required the labor of all available family members, and it is likely that all able-bodied women, men and children participated in various aspects of it. Ethnographic documentation shows that women and children are active in family-run vineyards, including those in Palestine in the early twentieth century CE. During harvest season, the whole family might move out to the vineyards and live in small stone structures built in the fields that served as guard houses, shelters and storage rooms (Amiry and Tamari 1989, 38). Several biblical passages specifically associate viticulture with women's work: Prov. 31.16 praises the righteous woman for her contributions in the vineyard and, in Song 1.6, the woman owns her own vineyard and laments that she could not work it herself (Walsh 2000, 59–61). Orah's family owned a vineyard that was only large enough to meet its needs, so they spent a short time in June and July harvesting grapes and producing wine and other edibles from them. Although a jar of wine was kept aside for Orah's future wedding, it was only a symbolic gesture; wine could not be stored successfully for more than a year or so, and Orah's wedding wine would likely turn to vinegar before Orah's parents could make her marriage arrangements.

Menstruation and Purity

Since there are no firsthand accounts of a girl's first menstruation in ancient Israel, the details of this important event in Orah's life must be reconstructed from various sources. The Hebrew Bible says little about the facts of menstruation; the biblical writers were not so interested in the everyday hygienic habits of women, and were mainly concerned with the state of impurity that arose during this time. No artifacts, except for perhaps anklets (see below), have been identified in ancient Israel that directly relate to a woman's first menstruation, and there is no iconographic or other information that relates directly to menstruation practices and beliefs in the archaeological record. Some sources from Mesopotamia and Egypt shed light on ancient Israelite practices; when used in tandem with the biblical evidence, one can begin to piece together the events surrounding the first menstruation of an ancient Israelite girl.

There is one hint to a ritual act that may have accompanied the onset of menstruation in the Hebrew Bible: Judg. 11.30-40, the story of Jephthah's daughter. The passage reads: "And Jephthah made a vow to the Lord, and said, 'If you will give the Ammonites into my hand, then whoever comes out of the doors of my house to meet me, when I return victorious from the Ammonites, shall be the Lord's, to be offered up by me as a burnt offering'" (Judg. 11.30-31). When Jephthah returns home, his daughter is the first to come out to meet him; she agrees to be sacrificed in fulfillment of her father's vow, but only after spending two months in the mountains "to bewail my virginity" with her companions (Judg. 11.37). The next passage, Judg. 11.40, relates an otherwise unknown female ritual, when all the young women of Israel went to the mountains to lament Jephthah's daughter four days of every year. Some have suggested that this refers to a female initiation rite that signaled a young woman's readiness for marriage, but no corroborating evidence for this practice is known (Bohmbach 2000, 244).

First menstruation must have been an important event in a young woman's life, for it was the time when a girl was incorporated into the women's world; thus, the physical development of the young woman was a source of pride for girls in the ancient Near East (van der Toorn 1994, 49). In our story, Orah is permitted for the first time into the circle of menstruating women in her household, and her initiation includes baking and offering bread cakes to Astarte in a cult corner in the west room of the house. Until then, Orah had only been permitted to assist with the offerings made to this deity, but on the occasion of her first blood, she became a full participant.

Orah's mother gives her two bronze anklets to mark the arrival of her first period and her new marriageable status; these bangles will remain on her ankles until her death. A study of metal anklets from Late Bronze and Iron Age I tombs and artistic depictions of males and females wearing anklets revealed that pairs of anklets were an important marker of gender, and "may have been symbolically linked to idealised perceptions of fertility, femininity, familial protection, and nakedness in depictions of female figurines" (Green 2007, 304). When men are shown wearing pairs of anklets in Egyptian art, however, they are associated with bondage, defeat and subservience. The anklets themselves, which are undecorated and resemble ingots, might have even been used as currency, and female anklet-wearing in ancient Israel may represent male dominance and control (Green 2007, 303–4).

Although the Hebrew Bible does not provide many details about the reality of menstruation, Leviticus 15 relates that regular and abnormal female genital discharge was considered unclean and that menstruating women were restricted from participating in public religious activity during that time (Lev. 15.18-33); these purity regulations were written much later than the Iron Age I period, however.[1] Specifically, menstruation resulted in a seven-day period of impurity when a woman could not enter the sanctuary. The menstruating woman and the objects under her could transfer impurity, and anyone who touched her or these objects would experience a one-day period of impurity and would be compelled to wash themselves and their clothes. If a man engaged in intercourse with a menstruating woman he was either impure for seven days (Lev. 15.24) or cut off from his people, along with the woman (Lev. 20.18). No passages indicate that women were isolated, and there was no specific need for sacrifice or ablutions at the end of the seven-day period; only the passage of time ended a woman's impure state.

There are other references to menstruation in the Hebrew Bible, notably two stories in Genesis: Genesis 18, where the text relates that "it had ceased to be with Sarah after the manner of women" (18.11) and Gen. 31.34–35, the story of Rachel's theft of her father's *teraphim*. Rachel's story provides some interesting information about the reality of female menstruation in the context of the ancient Israelite household. In this passage, after Rachel steals her father Laban's *teraphim* — household gods — and sits on them to hide them, she matter-of-factly tells her father that she cannot stand up when he enters the tent to search for them because "the way of women is upon me" (Gen. 31.35). This passage "might reflect a small and tight social group in which everybody knew which of the women menstruated, and when" (Philip 2005, 24), and it was perhaps not at all unusual for household members to discuss female menstruation. In addition, Laban did not find Rachel's reason for not standing up unusual or suspicious, so it may have been considered normal for a menstruating woman to be seated more than usual.

This story, which is believed to pre-date the purity legislation in Leviticus 15, may demonstrate an earlier train of thought in Israelite experience either concerning the impurity of menstruation (van der Toorn 1994, 52–53) or the connection between menstruation and fertility (Philip 2005, 19–25). Parallels with sources from Mesopotamia seem to confirm the aversion to menstrual blood and its impurity in a cultic context, but this may be more closely related to a widespread folk belief than to any intentional action on behalf of the priestly class to keep women out of cultic roles in ancient Israel. "Religiously, menstruation had an ambivalent character ... it was a sign of fertility and hence a blessing. But at the same time people regarded it as a source of impurity and this latter aspect is particularly emphasized in the ancient texts" (van der Toorn 1994, 49).

Since issues of purity apparently needed to be considered by menstruating women, it seems likely that women would have used some sort of protection during their periods and did not bleed out of their clothes as did many European and American women from the seventeenth to nineteenth centuries CE (Finley 2001). Although no archaeological evidence for them has been identified, the menstrual cloth (*beged idim*) is mentioned in Isa. 64.6. Menstruation is used as an image of impurity elsewhere in Isaiah (30.22) and in Lamentations, where a woman with unclean (bloody) skirts (Lam. 1.9) serves as a metaphor for Jerusalem after its destruction. There are several textual accounts from ancient Egypt that may refer to cloth menstrual pads as well (Robins 1993, 78).

In this story, scraps of wool felt and old rags were used by the women in Orah's household to absorb menstrual blood. Used rags were placed into a jar of water kept in the west room, where the cult corner was located, and every morning one or more of the menstruating women rinsed the cloths out for reuse. Once washed, the cloths would have dried quickly in the sun on the roof or in the courtyard. Plenty of vessels excavated at Iron Age I villages could have served purposes beyond those of cooking, serving and storing foods, and it is possible that such vessels as cooking pots and other open forms could have been used for soaking laundry, bathing and other activities related to hygiene. Basins that were apparently used for washing feet are mentioned in Pss. 60.8 and 108.9, and ceramic vessels that could have served this purpose have been found at Iron Age sites (see below).

Synchronous menstruation — the phenomenon of women living close together menstruating at the same time — has been documented ethnographically and can be assumed to have occurred in the four-room houses of early Israel. Such a situation must have fostered a sense of community among the women of a household. However, there is no evidence to suggest that women were fully secluded during menstruation in Iron Age I Israel. The purity laws in Leviticus do not stipulate that women live separately from men during menstruation; they instead regulate menstruation's relation to the cult and the holy (Philip 2005, 43). Although it is possible that women had to be attentive to issues of purity, and were perhaps restricted from sexual relations with men and from handling their personal belongings, it is unlikely that the household would have functioned without five to seven days of female labor each month.

It has been suggested that certain features of the Israelite four-room house were intended to accommodate times of ritual impurity, as this house plan gave maximum privacy to family members. The direct access permitted particularly to the rear rooms of the four-room house may have been designed to accommodate female impurity during menstruation. Since each room on the ground floor could be entered through the main room of the first floor directly, without having to pass through adjacent rooms, menstruating women did not have to leave the house at the times when they were ritually impure. It is possible that the plan was adopted to accommodate purity laws, or purity laws were structured by the house plan (Bunimovitz and Faust 2003, 415–17).

In our story, the menstruating women sleep separately from the men; when it is bearable, they sleep in the west room on the main floor, and when it is too hot they take their bedding to the courtyard and sleep there while the rest of the family sleeps on the roof or in the vineyard. But they are not completely secluded or cut off from the men in the family, and they still go about most of their daily activities as usual. During this time, we might imagine that children and older adults take on more responsibilities in the household; this is seen in our story when everyone but the women clean up after the evening meal and take charge of the children at bedtime.

Although the Hebrew Bible does not stipulate ritual cleansing after menstruation, later rituals, such as immersing oneself in a *mikveh* as a means of purification, may have their origins in earlier practices. Although only the passage of time was required for women to reenter normal life after menstruation, ritual bathing may have been practiced as for similar states of impurity, like seminal emissions (Lev. 15.16-18) or irregular/excessive vaginal bleeding (Lev. 15.28) (Burnette-Bletsch 2000, 205).

Men and women rarely changed their clothing or bathed completely in ancient Israel, although bathing in rivers is attested in the Hebrew Bible (2 Kgs 5.10-14). It is likely that hands, face and feet (Gen. 18.4; 19.2; 24.32; 43.24; Judg. 19.21; 1 Sam. 25.41) were washed more regularly as part of the ritual of hospitality and for reasons of purity. Bathing installations are not found in the Iron Age I village houses, but a clay figurine of a woman bathing in a small bathtub from seventh-century BCE Akhziv on the northern coast of Israel suggests bathtubs did exist (Figure 3.1), and ceramic basins featuring what may be a footrest and a spout for draining water have been found at eighth–seventh century BCE Samaria and at other sites (Dayagi-Mendels 1989, 14). In our story, Orah and Adah bathe in the spring outside of the village at the end of their periods to clean and perhaps purify themselves. As bathing outdoors was a rarity in ancient Israel, it would have been a treat for the young women that they looked forward to all month.

Perfume and Incense

Since bathing was limited in ancient Israel, perfume was considered to be more than just a luxury; in the hot, dry climate characteristic of much of the region, perfumes and unguents (oil-based ointments) would have provided protection and relief for skin parched by the sun. "Perfume and incense make the heart glad," according to Prov. 27.9, and a variety of different types of perfumes and incense are attested in the Hebrew Bible. Incense had sacred and profane functions in ancient Israel, and was used for divine worship, in funerals, for cosmetic purposes and as medicine. In our story, Orah's aunt burns incense in the cult corner in the west room for Astarte on the night of Orah's first period; the incense probably had the dual purpose of securing the

3.1 Woman bathing (after Vamosh 2007, 31).

presence of the deity to insure that the women's prayers reached her (Nielsen 1992, 406–7) and fumigating the small room where the menstruating women were spending the evening. On the day after her first period, Orah's mother gives Orah a small bottle of perfume, presumably to mask the odor of her menstruation.

Perfume was used "in religious ritual, burial preparation, personal groom-ing, healing, and a variety of other circumstances" (King and Stager 2001, 280). Oil was used as the base in perfumes in the ancient Near East, and olive oil would have been the most widely available liquid base for blend-ing in ancient Israel. Many kinds of plants are mentioned in the Hebrew Bible that could have been used to make perfumes and unguents. Only a few — henna, saffron, balm and ladanum — were native to the area, which means that balsam, frankincense, myrrh, cinnamon and others were imported from distant lands, usually in Africa and Asia. Flowers, leaves, branches, fruits and resin could be used in the production of perfume; resin was the most expensive of all these raw materials (Dayagi-Mendels 1989, 90–96).

The preparation of perfumes requires specialized skills, and it appears that certain groups controlled perfume production in specialized contexts. 1 Chronicles 9.30, for example, states that some of the priests' sons made ointment, presumably for use in the Temple. Women also apparently specialized in making perfumes for the palace, as suggested in 1 Sam. 8.11-13: "He said, 'These will be the ways of the king who will reign over you . . . [h]e will take your daughters to be perfumers and cooks and bakers.'" Cold steeping (enfleurage) and hot steeping (maceration) methods are attested in the ancient world, but there is a rather simple method of making perfume that was practiced early and by non-specialists: pressing. Aromatic plant parts could be crushed with a pestle in a mortar or other container or squeezed in twisted cloth to extract the fragrance (Dayagi-Mendels 1989, 96–97). Since oil-based preparations seem to have been necessary for everyday use in ancient Israel, they were either imported or produced by basic means during the Iron Age I. Balm, which most identify as *Balanites aegyptiaca*, grows in the Dead Sea and Jordan Valley (Dayagi-Mendels 1989, 107) and might have been available in the market in the village where Orah's father traded periodically.

The biblical writers describe the use of incense in divine worship. In the Tabernacle and, later, in the Temple in Jerusalem, an incense altar or burner was situated between the priest and the image of the deity. The purpose of regular morning and evening offerings of incense was to secure the presence of Yahweh and his attention in the hope that the fragrant odor would appease him, although the smoke could also provide a protective cover against divine wrath (Lev. 16.12-13) or the medium for the appearance of the deity (Lev. 16.2) (Nielsen 1992, 406–7). Incense also served to dispel unpleasant odors and to rid the sanctuary of flies and mosquitoes (King and Stager 2001, 346). It was also offered to gods other than Yahweh (1 Kgs 11.8; 2 Chron. 34.25; Jer. 48.35; Hos. 2.13), and it is likely that Israelite worship of Astarte involved the burning of incense. King Solomon reportedly worshiped Astarte (1 Kgs 11.5) and built holy sites around Jerusalem for the worship of various deities to whom his wives offered incense (1 Kgs 11.7-8).

Archaeological evidence for burning incense consists mainly of so-called incense burners and altars made of clay and stone that have been recovered from Iron Age sites. Some of these have physical evidence for burning on them, but many of them do not and it is possible that they served some other ritual function, perhaps as stands for offerings. Although most of the excavated examples have been identified in Iron Age II contexts, several have been found in the highlands that date to the Iron Age I. The best-known incense burner comes from a twelfth-century BCE cult room at 'Ai; it is in the form of a tall fenestrated (windowed) ceramic stand featuring decorative lion feet protruding near its base. It was found sitting on a bench near a bowl decorated with a circle of clay protuberances, a chalice-shaped stand, a lamp and other vessels. A clay animal figurine and a necklace with stone and glass beads were found inside the stand (Willett 1999, 203–4). Later altars — such as a fifth-century BCE example from Lachish — are inscribed with the names of the spices presumably burned on them in household rituals. The small stone altar from Lachish is inscribed with the Aramaic word for frankincense (Dayagi-Mendels 1989, 116–18).

Two of the most important ingredients of the incense used in the Tabernacle (Exod. 30.34) were frankincense and myrrh. Frankincense grew mainly in the southeastern region of the Arabian Peninsula, and myrrh came from Southwest Arabia and North Somalia (Dayagi-Mendels 1989, 116–18). This region was also a source of materials brought from India and China, such as the cinnamon required for anointing oil (Exod. 30.23) (Nielsen 1992, 407–8). The importation of these materials from South Arabia is confirmed by biblical and archaeological evidence. Isaiah 60.6 states: "A multitude of camels shall cover you . . . all those from Sheba shall come. They shall bring gold and frankincense, and shall proclaim the praise of the Lord." The Queen of Sheba, from South Arabia, brought "camels bearing spices" (1 Kgs 10.2) when she came to Jerusalem to visit Solomon. Archaeological evidence for this spice trade might be seen in seventh–sixth century BCE potsherds with incised inscriptions in South Arabian script found at Jerusalem and other sites (Dayagi-Mendels 1989, 114–16). Mesopotamian and Egyptian sources also shed light on the vast network of land and sea routes that existed in the Near East and Eastern Mediterranean for the trade in perfumes and spices in the second and first millennia BCE.

Household Religion

In our story, the goddess Astarte plays an important role in Orah's transformation from girl to young woman. Worshiping Astarte is just one facet of the household religion practiced in Orah's village and in the Iron I villages generally. Although the Hebrew Bible includes descriptions of the sanctuary at Shiloh (Chapter 6) that housed the Tabernacle and archaeological excavations have unearthed evidence for public worship in pilgrimage or village sanctuaries at a number of sites (Nakhai 2001, 176), the primary locus for religious worship in early Israel was the household (Meyers 2005, 60), and household ritual was the realm in which Israelite women could participate most fully in cult worship. Textual evidence from the ancient Near East suggests that household cults were often the province of women, and the family cult was very important to the maturing girl (van der Toorn 1994, 45). Although they were condemned by the writers of the Hebrew Bible during the monarchic period, household ritual activities were widespread in Israel throughout the Iron Age.

Household religious practices, like other expressions of "popular" religion, lie "outside the borders of the established cult and [are] located in the region of popular superstition where individuals perform actions that they cannot or will not introduce into the formal cult" (Zevit 2001, 662). Early Israelite household cult activities probably centered on "table manners" or the ritual actions that take place around meals, including offering a portion of food and drink to the gods (van der Toorn 1994, 30, 36) who may be physically present in the house in the form of *teraphim*, the household gods like those stolen by Rachel from her father. Later manifestations of these practices are described in the context of Temple ritual in the Hebrew Bible, including the idea that offerings are considered nourishment for Yahweh and the burnt offerings were a pleasing odor for him (Num. 28.24). Deuteronomy 4.28 criticizes acts of family piety that include worshiping gods of wood and stone, and "the reference to their inability to eat or smell indicates that people were in the habit of offering them food and incense" (van der Toorn 1994, 36).

The household cult required the use of a variety of common and specialized items. The archaeological remains of such practices include "those artifacts and ceramic vessels which are present in uncontested shrine sites, but may also appear in a domestic setting as evidence of religious activities practised by family members in the home" (Daviau 2001, 199). Archaeological evidence for household worship has been identified in village households in the Iron I, including Khirbet Raddana (Nakhai 2001, 173–74) and Tell Masos (Willett 1999, 107–17); more evidence is available for household cult practice in Iron Age II houses.[2] It has been argued that women controlled the space required for household economic activities such as baking and textile production in Iron Age I Israel, and it follows that women controlled certain cultic activities — especially those related to reproduction — practiced in the house as well (Meyers 2005, 68–69). The annual rite of lamenting Jephthah's daughter described in Judg. 11.40, although apparently not practiced in the house itself, may be an example of a ritual event carried out only by women, specifically, unmarried women (Meyers 2000a, 244–45).

In one room of an eleventh–tenth-century BCE house at Tell Masos in the Negev, artifacts of the household cult include clay incense burners and lamps, shells from the Red Sea, an ivory lion head and a bead. Based on Mesopotamian and Egyptian parallels as well as modern ethnographic data, it has been suggested that a woman with a newborn child slept in this room and protected herself and her newborn with the ivory figurine, shells and beads and by burning oil and incense. More artifacts and installations of a cultic nature were found in other parts of this house, including four female figurines similar to votives left in the temple to the Egyptian goddess Hathor at Timna, on the border between Israel and Egypt (Willett 2008, 90). Although we cannot know for certain if the Tell Masos figurines represent Hathor, their presence suggests "that the residents of this house at Tell Masos had an established relationship with a personal protective goddess that they worshiped in their home in addition to or instead of in a public sanctuary" (Willett 1999, 107–10).

Although there is no direct connection between the worship of Astarte and any known coming-of-age rites in ancient Israel, the goddess' primary role as a fertility deity makes her a logical choice of actor in this story. The mythology of this Canaanite goddess is best known from the texts found at the Syrian coastal city of Ugarit dating to the end of the second millennium BCE. Astarte was worshiped through the second millennium and into the first millennium BCE in Israel and Judah, as the biblical passages attest (Judg. 2.13; 10.6; 1 Sam. 7.3-4, 12.10; 1 Kgs 11.5, 33; 2 Kgs 23.13). According to the Late Bronze Age Ugaritic texts, Astarte was a divine courtesan, and sometimes the deity El's lover. She is referred to as "queen" in the first millennium BCE, and her cult involved baking and offering cakes (Ackerman 1992, 26).

The "queen of heaven" mentioned in Jeremiah (7.18; 44.19) and worshiped in Judah and Jerusalem in the sixth century BCE may be a syncretistic deity incorporating Astarte and the east Semitic goddess Ishtar (Ackerman 1989, 116–17). The prophet rails against pouring libations, burning incense and baking cakes as sacrifices to this goddess. According to Jer. 7.18, the cult is family oriented: "The children gather wood, the fathers kindle fire, and the women knead dough, to make cakes for the queen of heaven; and they pour out drink offerings to other gods, to provoke me to anger." Jeremiah 44.21 "describes the cult as one practiced in past generations" (Ackerman 1989, 117), much earlier than the sixth-century BCE context of the prophet's writing. The prophet accuses the kings and princes of Judah of worshiping the queen (Jer. 44.17, 21) and it is possible that she was worshiped in the Jerusalem Temple (Ackerman 1989, 117).

Bread and cakes were common offerings to deities in the ancient Near East and Egypt, and the Hebrew Bible relates that Yahweh required regular offerings of bread (Lev. 24.5-9). There are no specific stipulations as to the type of bread to be offered except that it should be made of "fine flour." A particularly interesting aspect of the cakes for the queen of heaven mentioned in Jer. 44.19 is that they were made "marked with her image." It has been suggested that such bread might have been baked in molds resembling the goddess or an identifying symbol was stamped on the bread,[3] but the archaeological examples of clay molds and stamps, such as the one in Figure 3.2 from Iron Age Cyprus, neither support nor refute these suggestions.

In this story, Orah forms cakes in the image of the goddess to thank her for giving her the ability to bear children and to ask for the continued fertility of the female members of the household. Orah's aunt burns incense to Astarte to invoke the goddess so that the women's prayers of thanks can be heard,

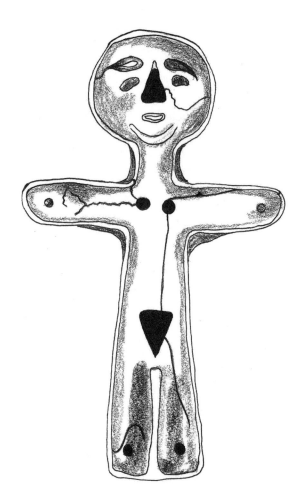

3.2 Bread mold (after King and Stager 2001, Ill. 23).

while other family members offer small token gifts in the form of beer and juice from the first grape harvest. Although other deities are worshiped by the members of Orah's household, Astarte has a special place in the lives of the women, and Orah's new relationship with the goddess will help her through the trials of childbirth in the future.

For Further Reading

Dayagi-Mendels, M. 1989. *Perfumes and Cosmetics in the Ancient World*. Jerusalem: The Israel Museum. A well-illustrated overview of perfumes and cosmetics in antiquity, including the implements and accessories used for their storage and application. A catalogue of the exhibition "Perfumes and Cosmetics in the Ancient World" at the Israel Museum.

McGovern, P. 2003. *Ancient Wine: The Search for the Origins of Viniculture*. Princeton: Princeton University Press. An engaging study of early wine and beer production in the ancient Near East, it includes a discussion of the earliest chemical evidence for wine and beer in the ancient world.

Meyers, C.L. 2005. *Households and Holiness: The Religious Culture of Israelite Women*. Minneapolis: Fortress Press. A brief, accessible discussion of the diversity of women's religious experiences and ritual participation in public and private contexts in ancient Israel.

Philip, T.S. 2005. *Menstruation and Childbirth in the Bible: Fertility and Impurity*. Studies in Biblical Literature 88. New York: Peter Lang. A study of the biblical texts concerning menstruation and childbirth, fertility and impurity in their ancient Near Eastern context.

van der Toorn, K. 1994. *From Her Cradle to Her Grave: The Role of Religion in the Life of the Israelite and the Babylonian Woman*. Trans. Sara J. Denning-Bolle. Sheffield: Sheffield Academic Press. A primarily text-based study of women's religious lives in the ancient Near East and ancient Israel "from cradle to grave."

Notes

1 Much of Leviticus is assigned to the Priestly tradition, which many scholars believe to be exilic (written down after 586 BCE). Thus, the purity regulations in Leviticus may not be applicable to highland village life in the early Iron Age.

2 See further Nakhai 2001, Willett 1999, 2008, and Zevit 2001.

3 See discussion in Hadley 2000, 41–42.

Chapter 4

Marriage

Orah's Story

Orah first saw her future husband on the pilgrimage to Shiloh when she was 12 years old, just after her sister Adah's wedding. Although families from nearby villages might make the long annual journey to Yahweh's most important shrine together, there was not much interaction between unrelated members of the opposite sex on such occasions and Orah did not actually speak to the young man. Orah's father and uncles happened to know him and his father, however, and her father pointed out the young man to Orah and her mother as they walked alongside his family. Although he did not say it aloud, her father believed that he might make a good husband for Orah in a few years.

Two years passed before Orah saw him again at Shiloh. She again did not speak to him, but this time she took notice of how tall he was, and how his green eyes stood out against his dark brown skin. And she could certainly not ignore the gossiping in her family's tent the first night of the festival; her father and mother had been discussing this tall young man, and everyone in the family seemed to know it. Although Orah was intrigued by the man, who was admittedly good-looking, she was more interested in his sister, who appeared to be several years younger than Orah. If her parents arranged a marriage between herself and this man, Orah thought, at least she might have an ally in this young woman. She missed her older sister Adah terribly, and liked the idea of gaining a sister close to her own age.

One hot afternoon the following summer, Orah's parents summoned her from the garden and asked her to join them in the orchards nearby. As they walked through the rows of ripening fruit trees, Orah's father revealed that Orah was to be married to this man, and preparations for the wedding were already underway. Orah's parents seemed very happy about the arrangements, and Orah's father talked favorably of the man's village, which he had recently visited. Orah was immediately saddened by the prospect of having to leave her family so soon, but she knew that her parents wanted the best for her and had surely made a good match, as they had for Adah several years earlier.

Her parents asked what she thought of their decision, and Orah thought it best to make them happy by telling them how grateful and excited she was, even if she did not truly feel that way.

Within days Orah's house was buzzing with preparations for the upcoming wedding. One morning a man arrived at the house — her future father-in-law, she soon learned — and gave Orah a pair of small gold earrings in a red woolen pouch. She and her mother thanked him for the gift and showed him the multi-colored wool fabric, still fastened to the loom in the courtyard, which would be made into a wedding garment for Orah. Orah's mother kept her so busy during the following few weeks harvesting the summer fruit and finishing her wedding garment, and talked so excitedly about the upcoming wedding that Orah had little opportunity to ask her mother what it would feel like to leave the family and move into the house of a stranger. When the day came, the women in Orah's house and the surrounding households prepared an elaborate meal to be served in the courtyard that evening and shared by the entire village. Orah wore her gold earrings in her newly pierced ears and her beautiful new robe and tried to enjoy being the center of attention at the party, which featured much singing and dancing led by the women in her family. A celebration was also underway in the village of Orah's husband-to-be that night, but Orah would not learn this until the next day, when she would leave her birth home escorted by her father and move into her new husband's house.

The new wine flowed freely at the wedding meal, and most of Orah's family slept in the next day so they would be present for her departure. After the morning meal, Orah's mother and the concubine helped her put her wedding clothing back on and pack her other belongings into woven bags. Until the time came to leave her birth house with her father, Orah sat in the courtyard lamenting that she would soon leave her family forever to live with strangers. As Orah's father prepared to leave a few hours later, her mother, aunt, and the concubine cried and sang a farewell song while they kissed Orah and wished her luck in her new home and fertility in the years to come. Orah's father watched quietly as some of the villagers came to their doors to bless Orah as they left the village, and he could not control his tears as they walked through the orchards and received the well wishes of the rest of their community.

As they slowly walked through the fields in the direction of Orah's new husband's village, Orah's father reassured her that the young man and his family would take good care of her. Orah was mostly silent during the trip, lost in thought about everything she would miss from her old life, and apprehensive about what awaited her in her new life. A few hours later, as they approached the village, Orah and her father were greeted in the surrounding terraces by Orah's husband and his male relatives. Her father and the young man's father embraced and exchanged the remaining gifts, and Orah's father kissed his daughter and son-in-law as he made the gesture understood by the gods and Orah's new family that he agreed to transfer protection of his daughter to her new husband. As they approached the family's courtyard and her father prepared to leave, he hugged Orah and blessed her again, telling her how proud he was of her and how much she would be missed.

Orah's husband then took her hand and led her into the house so that their fathers could talk alone for a few minutes. As she walked into her new house Orah entered a new world; some aspects of the house were familiar to her, but it was different from her birth house in many ways. The women of the house were cooking the evening meal, and they stopped their work to greet the new bride with songs before offering her a bowl of wine. Orah's husband introduced her to the women before showing her the rest of the house and the family's orchards, while his young sister, who had been excitedly watching the proceedings, followed closely behind. Although hesitant about what lay in store for her as a new wife, Orah was glad to meet her new family and reassured by the calm manner of her new husband, who smiled at her often as they walked through the rows of ripening pomegranates.

Introduction

Considering how vital marriage was to ancient Israelite society, it is interesting that the first mention of marriage in the Hebrew Bible — Gen. 2.24 — does not describe the actual Israelite marriage pattern (Hamilton 1992, 560). The passage, which reads ". . . a man leaves his father and his mother and clings to his wife, and they become one flesh," was not the reality of many, if any, of the marriages described in the Hebrew Bible. As discussed in Chapter 1, a patrilocal residence pattern was the norm, where a wife moved to her husband's family's house upon marriage. In addition, the ancient Israelite extended family — the *bet 'ab* — is considered by some to have been patriarchal, meaning that authority was theoretically in the hands of the oldest male in the family; reckoning descent and transmitting property was patrilineal, meaning that it passed through the father's line; and the ideal marriage situation was monogamous, with one man marrying one woman. Although these marriage characteristics may have held true for the most part in ancient Israel, there were certainly many exceptions, as the biblical passages attest.

The Hebrew Bible is replete with images of the biblical woman as wife and mother; wives figure prominently in the patriarchal narratives in Genesis especially, with its many family stories and emphasis on creating a genealogical scheme. Being married was the expected situation of an adult woman in ancient Israel, and not being married was a source of humiliation (Isa. 4.1). There is no Hebrew word for wife; instead, the biblical writers used the common word for "woman" — *'isha* — while husbands were frequently called *ba'al*, or "lord." This may suggest that the husband-wife relationship was characterized by the wife's subordination, which may in part be a response to the wife always being an outsider in her husband's household, and someone "who maintained bonds of loyalty to her father's house and who might consequently be used by her kinsmen" (Bird 1997, 39). The ideal marriage in ancient Israel was endogamous, or made within the larger group (Gen. 24.1-4; Judg. 14.1-3); in the Iron I, this probably meant that a man and a woman from the same tribe would ideally be married. Marriage with foreigners was considered dangerous, as in the case of Solomon, whose many foreign wives worshipped deities other than Yahweh (1 Kgs 11.1-8).

There are several biblical passages that describe the characteristics of the ideal wife. Abigail, wife of Nabal and, later, David (1 Sam. 25.2-42), is described as intelligent, beautiful, discreet and loyal despite the stupidity of her husband Nabal. The book of Proverbs contrasts the good wife with the bad wife, but also stresses that the ideal marital relationship is harmonious, with both partners benefitting from each other. There are also examples of women counseling their husbands behind the scenes, such as when David's wife Bathsheba influenced the succession to the throne of Israel in 1 Kgs 1.17-21 (Marsman 2003, 147–49). Although marriage was essential in ancient Israel, the biblical writers do not provide nuanced accounts of husband-wife relationships, and so we must imagine that the reality of marital relations was more complex and varied than the text reveals.

Orah is 15 years old when her parents choose a husband who was perhaps eight to ten years older than she, and they make the wedding arrangements together with the young man's parents. Orah's consent is requested by her parents but it is not required; she chooses to accept the match, but she knows that her opinion matters little in this situation. Having seen her sister Adah married several years earlier, Orah understands that she is destined to leave her birth house and move to a new village within a few years of her first menstruation. She will probably spend the rest of her life in her husband's village, maintaining little contact with her birth family. The fact that Orah first saw her future husband during the pilgrimage to Shiloh is no coincidence, as celebrations, like harvest feasts, provided opportunities for young women and men to meet (van der Toorn 1994, 56–58). It is also fitting that her wedding takes place in midsummer when pomegranates — potent fertility symbols in ancient Israel — are harvested along with other fruits.

Marriage Arrangements

The Hebrew Bible, our primary source for reconstructing marriage arrangements and wedding customs in ancient Israel, does not provide clear guidelines for marriage. Arrangements were usually initiated by the parents (Gen. 24.4; 34.1-4; Exod. 2.21), and the first reference to parentally arranged marriage is when Hagar selects a wife for her son Ishmael from Egypt (Gen. 21.21). This story also demonstrates that women and men were married relatively young, as Ishmael must have been a teenager when his mother arranged his marriage (Hamilton 1992, 562), although sometimes men married when they were older.[1] There are a number of other instances in which women were directly involved in matchmaking (Gen. 24.28, 55; Num 36.6; 1 Kgs 2.17-18), showing that mothers had some authority in this matter. In other passages, men are directly involved in their own marriage negotiations, such as Samson, who demands that his parents arrange for his marriage to a Philistine woman (Judg. 14.1-4). Other special arrangements like levirate marriage — when a widow marries her dead husband's brother so that her husband's line may continue (see Chapter 7) — are also described by the biblical writers.

Even though mothers could be involved in marriage negotiations, the language used in the arrangements is male: a woman is given, taken, sent for, captured or even purchased in the case of a slave wife (Bird 1997, 39). There are biblical passages that depict women as chattel, such as Exod. 20.17, where wives, children, slaves and livestock are listed as a man's major possessions. Women are also described as war booty (Deut. 20.14; 21.10-14; 1 Sam. 30.2, 5, 22; 1 Kgs 20.3, 5, 7; 2 Kgs 24.15), and wives are counted along with concubines, silver and gold as an index of a man's wealth (1 Kgs 10.14–11.8). Women were not simply property that could be bought and sold, however, and nowhere is a man's absolute sovereignty over his wife indicated in the biblical text (Marsman 2003, 146).

An important part of the marriage arrangements was setting the dowry and the bride price. The dowry — *shiluchim* — was given by the bride to her new husband's family, and the bride price — *mohar* — was intended to compensate the bride's family for the loss of her economic contributions to her father's household. The dowry could include gifts of land, such as when Solomon married an Egyptian princess and was given the city of Gezer by her father, the pharaoh (1 Kgs 9.16); giving land was probably a practice reserved for royals and the wealthy, however. Unusual requests — such as when Saul asks David to bring a hundred Philistine foreskins for the hand of Saul's daughter Michal (1 Sam. 18.25) — are also described. Shechem offers Jacob anything he wants in exchange for his daughter Dinah after Shechem rapes and presumably falls in love with her (Gen. 34.12). More commonly, perhaps, jewelry was exchanged between the two families, such as in the story of Rebekah (Gen. 24.53); servants were also given as gifts (Gen. 29.24, 29). Exchanging gifts helped create or maintain the relationship between the two families, which would create mutual obligations in case one family needed assistance in the future (Meyers 1999a, 118).

The marriage arrangement was thus an agreement made between two families, and the wife's rights within the marriage would have depended on her family's ability to support her demands; thus the daughter of a rich or powerful man would have higher status than the daughter of a poor man, and could probably expect better treatment (Bird 1997, 38). Several biblical passages show that young brides were not totally passive or lacking initiative in the marriage arrangements, however (1 Sam. 18.20; 2 Sam. 11.2-5), and a woman could refuse an offer (Gen. 24.5; 57–58) or make demands (Judg. 1.14-15). When Rebekah's marriage with Isaac is being arranged, for example, Rebekah is asked by her mother and brother if she will go to Canaan to marry him willingly: "They said, 'We will call the girl, and ask her.' And they called Rebekah, and said to her, 'Will you go with this man?' She said, 'I will.'" (Gen. 24.57-58). After she agreed to marry Isaac, Rebekah and her nurse left for Canaan with Abraham's servant and his men.

Since most marriages were parentally arranged, how did love factor into it? Love and courting are found in the stories of Jacob and Rachel (Gen. 29.18-20) and Samson and Delilah (Judg. 16.4), and in normal practice a man takes the woman he loves as a wife (2 Sam. 13.1, 15-16). Men are typically the ones who actively love their wives, however, and the only time a woman is described as loving a man in the Hebrew Bible is when Saul's daughter Michal loved David (1 Sam. 18.20). In this case, it is a princess who is in love with a male commoner, making it acceptable. However, a wife's sexuality belonged exclusively to her husband and the law demanded that wives be virgins. If an unmarried girl is guilty of sex before marriage, it is a crime against her father; if she is married, it is a crime against her husband. "Adultery involving a married woman was a crime of first magnitude in Israelite law, ranking with murder and major religious offenses as a transgression demanding the death penalty — for both offenders" (Bird 1997, 24).

Although several passages state that a man who has sex with a married woman is to be killed (Lev. 20.10; Deut. 22.22), men were not restricted from relations with prostitutes (Gen. 38.15-19) and could also have multiple wives and concubines, as we have seen in our story.

Wedding Customs

Every society has customs and traditions that accompany a couple's transition to marriage. The biblical writers do not describe a specific wedding ceremony, but a number of activities that may have accompanied marriage are described or alluded to. The concept of engagement, for example, may be apparent in the story of Lot in Gen. 19.14, when the text states that Lot's sons-in-law are pledged to marry his daughters. This early stage in the marriage transition — the betrothal — could last several months, and some biblical passages treat betrothal and marriage almost the same (Deut. 28.30; 2 Sam 3.14) (King and Stager 2001, 54). A man might show intent for a woman by covering her with the corner of his mantle (Ruth 3.9; Ezek. 16.8); this action might equate to an oath or covenant expressed between a man and his intended bride. Gifts of jewelry might also show a man's intent, as when Rebekah is given a gold nose ring and two gold bracelets by Abraham's servant (Gen. 24.22). Bachelor parties may have been customary, as Samson had a seven-day feast that was only for the young men (Judg. 14.10). There are no recorded marriage contracts in the Hebrew Bible, but divorce contracts are mentioned, which could mean that marriage contracts also existed (Deut. 24.1; Isa. 50.1; Jer. 3.8). Marriage in ancient Israel had no religious component and was considered a civil contract (King and Stager 2001, 56).

There are no hints in the Hebrew Bible about what time of year weddings were typically celebrated, if there was such a time. According to Palestinian ethnography, "[i]f one has not celebrated the wedding after the wheat harvest at the end of May and beginning of June, one hastens to do it before winter sets in" (Granqvist 1935, 32). There may have been practical as well as symbolic reasons why a spring or summer wedding was preferable. Several biblical passages hint at the rituals that may have been performed at a wedding, such as Hos. 2.19-20, which might be a formula for a marriage ceremony: "And I will take you for my wife forever; I will take you for my wife in righteousness and in justice, in steadfast love, and in mercy. I will take you for my wife in faithfulness; and you shall know the Lord." Psalm 45 also gives some insight into the activities that may have accompanied a wedding

(King and Stager 2001, 55). We cannot know if these descriptions reflect the actual practices of the village population of the Iron I, however.

Farewell songs were apparently sung as a woman left her birth house for her husband's house, such as when Rebekah sets off for Canaan to marry Isaac: "And they blessed Rebekah and said to her, 'May you, our sister, become thousands of myriads; may your offspring gain possession of the gates of their foes'" (Gen. 24.60). What happens next to the newly married woman is not well-understood. In early twentieth-century Palestine, the mother of the bride accompanied her daughter to the husband's village: "[t]he mother of the bride — or if she is dead one of her nearest relatives — always goes with the bridal procession to see how things will be with her daughter in the husband's home . . . [she] stays ten-fifteen-twenty days or even a month until she has settled her daughter" (Granqvist 1931, 93). The biblical text offers no information about the events surrounding a woman's move to her new home, but we can imagine that her departure was very emotional for the woman and her family.

Once a woman married and moved to her husband's village, it was expected that she would live there for the rest of her life. Of course there were circumstances that led to less than ideal situations, such as early widowhood, and these were usually resolved by the husband's family. Divorce was probably infrequent in the early Iron Age, and if it occurred, it may have been a male prerogative (Deut. 24.1-4). The divorced or deserted wife would probably then return to her father's household, as did Samson's wife from Timnah (Judg. 15.1-2). Since a woman usually owned no property, she was reliant on her father before marriage and on her husband after (Bird 1997, 23) (see further Chapter 7).

In our story, Orah's wedding celebration takes place in her village and includes a big party where she is the center of attention in her new clothing and jewelry. When she is taken by her father to her husband's village the next day, her departure is marked by laments and songs by the members of her household and good-luck wishes from the other villagers. Upon arrival to her husband's village, she is greeted by her new family members and given a tour of her new house and its surroundings by her husband. Their walk through the pomegranate orchards hints to the fertility expected of the new couple, who would have been expected to consummate the marriage almost immediately with the hopes of having a child as soon as possible.

Music and Dancing

Music and dancing accompany Orah's wedding celebrations; both were important in various public and private, sacred and secular, events in ancient Israel. Women are specifically associated with music and dance in a number of passages in the Hebrew Bible, and artistic depictions of women playing instruments are known from Bronze and Iron Age sites in Israel and contemporary sites in Egypt and the ancient Near East. We learned in Chapter 3 that Orah's mother accompanied the group of singing women with a drum in the west room on the evening of Orah's first menstruation, and it is possible that simple instruments like drums were owned by the highland inhabitants of early Iron Age Israel, although their remains are usually difficult to detect.

The biblical writers provide many names for the instruments played in ancient Israel, and these instruments can be classified into four categories: chordophones (string instruments), aerophones (wind-blown instruments), membranophones (instruments with a stretched membrane) and idiophones (self-sounding instruments) (Burgh 2006, 8). Chordophones, like lyres and harps, are mentioned in various biblical passages and depicted in iconographic representations; one of the Hebrew Bible's most famous musicians — the young David — was brought to Saul's court to play the lyre to calm the troubled king (1 Sam. 16.14-23). Aerophones, which include pipes, double-pipes, flutes and trumpets, are similarly described in the biblical text and depicted in iconography, and the only archaeological remains of these instruments come from Egypt and Mesopotamia. Membranophones, such as drums and tambourines, were quite popular in ancient Israel, and may have been considered "women's instruments" (see below). Idiophones, including rattles and cymbals, are known from numerous archaeological examples as well as biblical descriptions and artistic representations.

Based on archaeological and textual evidence, it is possible and even likely that Israelite women played instruments from all four categories. On a ninth-century BCE ceramic storage jar from the desert site of Kuntillat 'Ajrud, a female figure seated on a throne plays the lyre; accompanying her in the scene are figures that some have interpreted as Yahweh and the goddess Asherah based partly on an accompanying inscription that reads: "I bless you by Yahweh of Samaria and by his asherah." An ivory carving from Late Bronze Age Tel el-Farah (south) may depict a woman playing a double-pipe; although the identification of the sex of this musician cannot be made definitively, there are many known Egyptian representations of women playing flutes and double-flutes (Burgh 2006, 50–56). Clay plaque figurines of women playing frame drums are known from several Iron Age sites in Israel, as are three-dimensional figurines of women playing the frame drum, like the one in Figure 4.1 from Shikmona on Israel's northern coast. Although iconographic depictions of rattles and cymbals in ancient Israel are scant, women are frequently depicted playing these instruments in ancient Egyptian art.

The Hebrew Bible includes a number of descriptions of women playing the drum, and this instrument may have been more closely associated with female musical performance than male musical performance. For example, Miriam, sister of Moses and Aaron, sang as she led a group of women in

4.1 Woman with hand drum (after Meyers 1988, cover illustration).

playing frame drums and dancing to celebrate victory over the Egyptians in Exod. 15.20-21, and Jephthah's doomed daughter greeted her father with drums and dancing in Judg. 11.34. In these and other passages, such as when Deborah and Barak sang on the day they defeated the Canaanite general Sisera (Judges 5), women participated in public musical performance specifically to celebrate victory in battle.

Women were musicians in public religious events as well. Several biblical passages describe musicians' guilds organized for the Jerusalem Temple (1 Chron. 6.31; 15.16-24; 25.1-8; 2 Chron. 35.15) that women participated in (2 Chron. 25.5-6). A large group of male and female cult singers also performed upon their return from the Exile (Neh. 7.67; Ezra 2.64-65), showing continuity in what appears to have been an ancient tradition (Meyers 1999b, 168).

When discussing music in the early Iron Age, however, we are most interested in women's musical performance in the household or village setting; unfortunately, there is not much information in the biblical text that informs on women's singing in the household or village context. We can imagine that women sang as they performed the monotonous tasks of grinding grain, making pottery and weaving, as documented in ethnographic descriptions (see Chapter 2). In the Hebrew Bible, singing also accompanied agricultural work shared by both sexes, such as the processing of grapes (Jer. 25.30; 48.33). The biblical writers specifically describe men singing while doing monotonous chores like digging a well (Num. 21.16-18). Although the women's farewell song on Orah's wedding day could be considered a public performance of sorts, it was really intended to celebrate this momentous occasion for Orah, and lament the loss of this important member of their household.

Dancing also accompanied many events in ancient Israel, as evidenced by the biblical descriptions as well as iconography on Iron Age seals and *bullae* (stamp seal impressions) and other ceramic art. In the Hebrew Bible, "[m]ainly dances were performed by women" (Mazar 2003, 126). As discussed above, women danced to celebrate military victory in the stories of Miriam and Jephthah's daughter; women also danced when greeting the victorious David (1 Sam. 18.6) and while celebrating the "yearly festival of the Lord" held at Shiloh (Judg. 21.19-22) (see Chapter 6). Dancing accompanied by music played a role in religious activities, such as when the Israelites danced around the golden calf (Exod. 32.19) and when David brought the Ark of the Covenant to Jerusalem (2 Sam. 6.5, 14-15). Iron Age seal impressions show figures with outstretched hands that may be dancing together, and the "Dancers Stand" from the Philistine site of Tel Qasile on Israel's southern coast, which dates to the Iron Age I, features figures with hands stretched out at their sides, moving in a line or in a circle in a clockwise direction (Mazar 2003, 127–29). Unfortunately, it is impossible to identify the sex of the dancers in these images.

It is possible that female dancing was segregated from male dancing in ancient Israel, since two different verbs for "dance" are used to describe female and male dancing in the Hebrew Bible. The verb used for female dancing implies that women danced in circles, and the verb used for male dancing implies that men jumped up and down, like grains bouncing in a sieve or ships bouncing on the waves (Ilan 2003, 136). It may be that women often participated in group dancing, and men in individual dancing; it is also possible that women danced for men and men danced for women, as dancing could have sexual overtones (Ilan 2003, 136). Such dancing would have been appropriate at Orah's wedding, since "dancing was mobilized as a means of courtship in ancient Israel" (Ilan 2003, 135), and wedding celebrations may have been events at which young men and women might meet and get to know each other. Informal female dancing in groups might have celebrated other important events in women's lives, such as a successful childbirth, or the birth of a boy specifically (see Chapter 5).

Clothing

Clothing items, which are made of organic material, do not tend to survive from ancient Israel except in the extraordinary preservation of woven material at desert sites, such as Kuntillat 'Ajrud (see Chapter 2). Accessories, most commonly the simple pins, toggle pins and fibulae made of metal or bone that fastened clothing in place, are commonly found in archaeological contexts, but they rarely accompany the remains of actual clothing items (Irvin 1997, 39). Information about clothing worn by women during the early Iron Age is thus drawn from biblical descriptions and a few contemporary iconographic depictions of Israelite women; we cannot assume, however, that this written and pictorial evidence represents the everyday clothing worn by the typical Israelite, especially those who lived in the highland villages. Nonetheless, we can begin to reconstruct how an ancient Israelite woman might have dressed based on the available evidence, and speculate that a woman might have worn a special garment on her wedding day, which was a transformative time that may have been marked with unusual clothing and adornment.

The many references to clothing and other forms of ornamentation in the Hebrew Bible, including jewelry (see Chapter 5), demonstrate the social and symbolic significance of clothing and adornment. The word for clothing, *beged*, appears over 200 times and refers to everything from a high priest's robe (Lev. 8.30) to a leper's torn garments (Lev. 13.45) (Edwards 1992, 232). Women and men wore much the same clothing although, according to Deut. 2.5, men were prohibited from wearing the *simla*, an article of clothing apparently worn only by women. Another specific clothing item worn by women was a sash or belt, which is mentioned in Isa. 3.24. Undergarments of some sort may have also been worn, although we lack information about such clothing items. The main garment worn by women was a *ketonet*, which was a long robe or tunic worn close to the skin. Princesses wore a *ketonet passim* according to 2 Sam. 13.18, the story of the rape of David's daughter Tamar by her brother Amnon. A *ketonet passim*, which is translated as a coat with long sleeves or a multicolored or striped coat, could also be worn by men, or at least young men, as Jacob gave his youngest son Joseph such a coat, apparently as a symbol of Jacob's favoritism (Gen. 37.3).

Like men, women wore some sort of outer garment over their *ketonet*; the abundance of terms for this outer garment in the Hebrew Bible, however, makes an understanding of these clothing items difficult (Edwards 1992, 232). Iconographic depictions provide the best evidence for what the outer garment — which was something like a mantle or cloak — would have looked like. Paintings on the walls of a nineteenth-century BCE Middle Kingdom tomb at Beni Hasan, Egypt, for example, include detailed, colorful depictions of Canaanite men, women and children, along with their animals (Pritchard 1969, figure 3). The four women depicted in this relief are shown wearing calf-length garments of colored cloth with colorful and complex woven designs that leave the right shoulder and both arms bare. This garment was held in place with a pin at the shoulder. The women also wear headbands to hold their long hair in place and closed shoes with tops that reach above the ankle that are probably made of leather (Irvin 1997, 39–40); evidence for the footwear worn by Israelite women is scarce, although Song 7.1 describes a woman wearing sandals. The wall paintings from Beni Hasan might reflect the kinds of outer garments worn by later Israelite women as well, although it is impossible to be sure given the dearth of colored images and detailed textual descriptions that have survived.

Among the other depictions of Israelite — or, more accurately, Judean — women are images from Assyrian art. Images of captive women and men from the city of Lachish in Judah are preserved on the walls of the Assyrian king Sennacherib's palace at Nineveh, in Iraq; these images record the conquest of Lachish by Sennacherib in 701 BCE. In scenes carved in relief on large stone wall panels, women and girls from Lachish wear long cloaks pulled up over their heads like hoods and no shoes (see Figure 4.2). The wall reliefs from Sennacherib's palace are particularly important because they are definitely depictions of Judean women as opposed to female deities, and they include the only known representations of Judean children. Although they were recorded by Assyrian artists who accompanied Sennacherib on his military expedition to Lachish, the accuracy of the rendering of the city and its fortifications is generally supported by archaeological excavations at the site (Ussishkin 1982) and we might assume that the artists gave a reliable rendering of the female deportees as well. The rendering of women from different regions in the Near East with distinctive dress, headgear and

4.2 Women from Lachish (after Ussishkin 1982, Fig. 70).

hairstyles in these and other Assyrian reliefs may also support this assumption (Albenda 1983).

An interesting *ostracon* (a piece of inscribed pottery) dating from the seventh century BCE from the site of a fortress at Mesad Hashavyahu, near the coast of southern Israel, demonstrates the value of clothing in ancient Israel. In this inscription, which was apparently dictated to a scribe, a field worker appeals to the governor of the fortress for the return of an item of clothing that he complains had been unjustly confiscated by a man named Hoshabyahu ben-Shobi. Although the item of clothing is not specified, it was probably a mantle or cloak given its apparent worth to the worker. The reason for the confiscation of this man's garment is unknown, and the worker professes to be innocent of any wrongdoing (Albright 1976, 121). Clearly, this clothing item was considered valuable to the field worker, and he took the necessary steps to attempt to get it back. Whether his clothing was returned, however, is unknown.

Specialized articles of clothing were worn by women to denote status and position. According to the Hebrew Bible, a woman would wear a veil, *sa'ip*, to cover her face on her wedding day (Gen. 24.65); women wore veils in public on other occasions as well (Isa. 3.18-20; 47.2). Psalm 45, "Ode for a Royal Wedding," describes the rich garment worn by a wealthy woman on her wedding day: "The princess is decked in her chamber with gold-woven robes; in many-colored robes she is led to the king" (Psalm 45.13-14). As we have seen, princesses and other royal women might have been distinguished from others by special garments, as in the case of Tamar in 2 Sam. 13.18.

Women in early twentieth-century Palestine wore a new embroidered dress and jacket as a wedding outfit; because of their great value, these were considered the most important items that the bride would bring to her husband's family (Granqvist 1981, 76). On her wedding day, Orah wears a special woolen robe with multicolored threads that she and her mother have woven especially for this event; this garment could have been part of the dowry that she brings with her to her new home. Her new robe and the gold earrings given to her by her father-in-law clearly mark her as a new bride during the feast held in her honor in her birth village, and the next day, when she enters her husband's household for the first time.

For Further Reading

Braun, J. 2002. *Music in Ancient Israel/Palestine: Archaeological, Written and Comparative Sources*. Grand Rapids, MI: Eerdmans. A comprehensive study of the sources for understanding music in ancient Israel from prehistory through the Roman period, with a special focus on the archaeological evidence.

Burgh, T. 2006. *Listening to the Artifacts: Music Culture in Ancient Palestine.* New York: T&T Clark International. An investigation into the evidence for music in Iron Age Israel that specifically considers women's participation in musical performance.

Hamilton, V.P. 1992. Marriage: Old Testament and Ancient Near East. In *Anchor Bible Dictionary*, vol. 5, ed. D.N. Freedman. New York: Doubleday, 559–69. A concise overview of the evidence for marriage customs and practices in the ancient Near East and in the Hebrew Bible.

Marsman, H.J. 2003. *Women in Ugarit and Israel: Their Social and Religious Position in the Context of the Ancient Near East.* Leiden: Brill. Compares the position of women in the literary texts from Bronze Age Ugarit with the status of women in the Hebrew Bible. This book also discusses women's roles in the family and in society, and as religious specialists and worshipers.

Note

1 Such as Esau, who married at age 40, and Joseph, at age 30 (Borowski 2003, chapter 4, note 52).

Chapter 5
Childbirth

Orah's Story

Orah was terrified of what was to come. She was very hot in the confines of the rear room of the house in the late summer afternoon, and already exhausted from hours of labor. She had been pregnant twice before, but had lost both fairly early on and was convinced that something would go wrong now as well. Orah had witnessed many births during her 18 years and had seen one woman die in childbirth, and she knew full well it could happen to her. She was somewhat comforted by the midwife — an older woman from the village who had helped many women give birth before — and by the presence of her two sisters-in-law and mother-in-law. She especially appreciated her older sister-in-law's calmness, and trusted her experience as the mother of two young children. As Orah walked around the small room, stopping every few minutes for a contraction, the women recited spells to ward off the demons that threatened Orah and her baby; meanwhile, the midwife burned incense on the shrine in the corner of the room and beseeched the gods for protection during this dangerous time.

To take her mind off the pain, Orah thought back to the previous few weeks, when she had spent much of her time harvesting the last of the summer fruits in the orchard with the rest of her household. Orah had tried to carry the heavy baskets of pomegranates and figs on her head back to the house as she had always done, but she had a hard time balancing them and had to allow her young sister-in-law to carry them for her. Since she could not contribute to the household chores as much as usual, and her mother-in-law kept telling her to rest in the shade and not push herself so much, she spent hours weaving baskets and mats in the relative coolness of the shelter built in the corner of the courtyard against the front of the house. In the week before the birth, she was able to complete a large basket that would be used as a cradle for the new baby; she had been saving up the stalks of wheat since the spring harvest just for this occasion. She had a lot of experience weaving baskets and mats and found the repetition of this activity relaxing. The thought of the cradle, which sat in one corner of the room awaiting the baby's arrival, comforted her a bit, as did the familiar weight of the eye pendant that hung on a cord around her neck.

When Orah's contractions finally came close together and her moans made it clear that the baby would soon be born, the midwife took the two clay birth bricks stacked in a corner and placed them in the middle of the room. Before Orah was to kneel on them, the midwife piled several layers of cloth on top to make them more comfortable. As Orah knelt down on the bricks and began pushing, the women helped to support her and they said their prayers more loudly whenever Orah yelled out in pain. Finally, after the head appeared and it was clear that the baby would soon be born, the midwife and the women of the household talked excitedly among themselves and assured Orah that the end was near. After the baby emerged, and the women saw that it was a boy, they shouted and danced around the room as the midwife helped Orah off of the bricks and onto a mat on the floor nearby while she held the bloody newborn in one arm. The midwife then rubbed the crying infant with salt, cut the cord, wrapped him in strips of wool and handed him to Orah's mother-in-law. The midwife then helped Orah deliver the afterbirth, which she wrapped in a piece of cloth; later, she would bury it in the dirt floor under the entrance to the room to help prevent evil forces from entering the space.

After the midwife and the older sister-in-law helped Orah clean up a bit and get comfortable on a cushion propped against the wall, Orah's mother-in-law brought the baby to Orah to hold. Unable to believe that this perfect baby was really her son, Orah cried as she asked her sister-in-law to send one of her own children to the orchards to tell her husband the good news. Her husband had been the first in the house to learn very early in the morning that Orah felt the cramping that meant the baby would soon arrive, and he had been excited and nervous all day as he awaited news of what happened in the birthing room. As her young niece was sent with the news, Orah and the other women talked about names for the child; it was the tradition in her husband's family — as it had been in her own — for women to name the babies, and Orah had several names in mind. Soon after, Orah's husband came running into the house, shouting with joy at the good news. He entered the rear room, kissed his wife and took the baby to show the rest of the family, who were following shortly behind him. Thankful that both his wife and son were doing well, he said a quiet prayer of thanks to the gods for their blessing and promised Yahweh that he would bring an appropriate sacrifice to his shrine at Shiloh during the upcoming pilgrimage.

After everyone had a chance to admire the new baby, Orah's husband brought him back to the rear room for Orah to nurse. As Orah and the baby got comfortable, her husband tied a string of blue beads around the baby's neck before being sent from the room by the women, who wanted to finish cleaning and attend to the new mother. As night fell and the rest of the family gathered in the courtyard to eat the evening meal that had been prepared by her younger sister-in-law, Orah placed her son in his new basket cradle and ate the bowl of porridge that her mother-in-law brought to the rear room. She then lay down on the mat to rest until the baby woke up ready to be fed again.

A few days later, after Orah had recovered a bit, she named the baby and her husband had him circumcised according to the customs of the village. Everyone in the village attended the event, which was held in the courtyard and accompanied by a great feast prepared by the women in Orah's house. Orah came out into the courtyard only briefly during the celebration; it was expected that she would spend these postpartum days in the rear room to regain her strength and her purity. The birth of a son had instantly elevated her status in the village, and she gratefully accepted the gestures of blessing from her female neighbors. That evening as she sat, alone, in the rear room, she burned incense next to a clay figurine of Astarte and thanked the gods who had permitted this miracle to happen.

Introduction

We know nothing of the consummation of marriage in ancient Israel, although we can imagine that it took place soon after the bride moved into her husband's family's house. After all, the primary responsibility of women — and of men, for that matter — was to be fruitful and multiply (Gen. 1.28). A large family, especially a family with many sons, was ideal, and it was absolutely essential in the agrarian households of the Iron Age I (Meyers 1997, 27). Children were considered a blessing, and the biblical writers compared barrenness to being dead (Gen. 30.1) and a result of divine punishment or displeasure (Gen. 16.2; 20.18; 1 Sam. 1.5; 2 Sam. 6.23). According to ethnographic sources in Palestine, the idea that successful births are the result of God's intervention persisted into the twentieth century; according to one informant, "[i]t is important for a woman to bear a child, especially important to bear a son, but in this respect she is in God's hands. Particularly when a woman is barren does she feel wholly dependent on His grace" (Granqvist 1931, 34).

A barren woman was deprived of the honor attached to motherhood, which, in ancient Israel, was the only position of honor generally available and the highest status most women could achieve (Bird 1997, 35–36). Barrenness threatened a woman's status as a wife (Gen. 30.1-2, 15), and motherhood brought with it the chance for a woman to exercise power over another person. This must have been a factor in a woman's desire for children since "the only relationship in which dominance by the woman was sanctioned was the mother-child relationship" (Bird 1997, 36). The Hebrew Bible includes a number of examples of a woman's control over her son (Gen. 21.10; 27.46–28.2; Judg. 14.3; 1 Kgs 1.15-20) and it is clear that a woman's status increased upon the birth of a boy. Women would have also prized their daughters, however, in part for their important economic contributions to the household and the assistance they provided their mothers (see Chapter 2).

Pregnancy itself is hardly described by the biblical writers, and the only time the biblical text focuses on a woman who is pregnant but not in labor is when Rebekah asks Yahweh questions about her apparently difficult pregnancy (Gen. 25.22) (Gursky 2001, 43). The biblical writers were either not familiar with the experiences of pregnant women or did not consider them important enough to discuss in detail. Outside of the Hebrew Bible, Iron Age images of pregnant women can be found in the art of Israel's neighbors, particularly in Phoenicia. A figurine from Akhziv depicting a pregnant woman sitting on a chair with her feet on a stool, wearing an Egyptian-style wig and resting a hand on her large stomach (see Figure 5.1) may have been used by women to promote fertility or success in childbirth. Otherwise, we have very little archaeological information that directly informs on pregnancy. There is a bit more information in the biblical text about childbirth itself, although we must still look to other textual sources from the ancient Near East and Egypt and the available ethnographic sources to reconstruct a more complete picture of birthing customs in ancient Israel.

Midwives

Until very recently in the West, midwives or female family members attended most births in the home or in a healthcare establishment. Evidence from the Hebrew Bible and other Near Eastern and Egyptian sources indicate that births were often attended by midwives or other experienced women in the ancient world. Childbirth is thus an activity that was almost assuredly outside the realm of most men's experience, and was not an event that required the intervention of more established medical practitioners, even when they existed. The childbirth event is thus unique among daily-life activities in

5.1 Pregnant woman (after Vamosh 2007, 45).

ancient Israel because it was experienced by female experts and women in groups, who had full control over the process. Midwifery was one of the very few female professions that gave women the opportunity to meet other women, teach novices and gain respect for their skills in the community (Meyers 2000b, 183).

Despite their important jobs, midwives are mentioned only three times in the Hebrew Bible. In Gen. 35.17, Rachel gives birth on the way to Ephrath/ Bethlehem and is attended by a midwife; she dies soon after giving birth to a son, Benjamin. Tamar gives birth to twin boys by her father-in-law Judah in Gen. 38.28 with the aid of a midwife, who ties a red thread around the wrist of the first baby to emerge and names the second one Perez, "breech." Exodus 1.15-21 describes the actions of two named midwives — Shiphrah and Puah — who are instructed by Pharaoh to kill all of the Israelite boys they deliver and allow the girls to live, but the two women intentionally defy Pharaoh by allowing all of the children they deliver to live. Women could also be assisted in childbirth by women in the community (Ruth 4.16-17); the neighborhood women who assist Ruth in the birth of her son Obed also name the child.

The midwife in ancient Israel was an important healthcare practitioner, but she was also a source of emotional support and a ritual expert. In Gen. 35.17, when Rachel apparently expresses fear during her difficult labor, the midwife comforts her by saying, "Do not be afraid; for now you will have another son." The midwife who assisted Tamar ties a red thread around the wrist of the first baby to emerge; the thread serves not only to prove which was the firstborn son, but it also had amuletic powers. Archaeological evidence and comparative textual material demonstrate that figurines and jewelry items were used to ensure the safety of the newborn and the mother. Rubbing salt on a newborn, an activity performed by midwives, and naming the baby, the responsibility of women more often than men in the Hebrew Bible, also may have had ritual meaning (see below).

The biblical references do not provide much information about the women who served as midwives, except for the story of Shiphrah and Puah. According to Exod. 1.20-21, Yahweh was so pleased with the work of these midwives that he not only increased the number of the Hebrews and their power, but also gave the midwives families of their own. This may suggest that the midwives had been previously barren and still young enough to bear children (Gruber 2000a, 138). This is interesting since midwives, then as today, are usually older women who have given birth themselves. According to Palestinian ethnography, a midwife should be so old that she has ceased to menstruate and will never again be impure; as an older woman, she has only seriously begun to fast and pray, and she gains more respect as a "mother" than a younger woman (Granqvist 1931, 61). In our story, the midwife who assists the birth is an older woman who has borne several children and assisted in the births of many others in Orah's husband's community and the surrounding villages. Her role is not only to help ensure the successful birth of Orah's child, but also to comfort Orah and perform the rituals required to invoke the gods for protection and keep harmful forces at bay.

In the Hebrew Bible, the woman-in-childbirth motif "has fixed the poet's attention" (Bird 1997, 35). For the biblical writers, birth pangs were the greatest anguish known, and metaphors related to the pain, helplessness and fear experienced by women during childbirth are contrasted with the experiences of a warrior (Jer. 30.6). Thus, the image of a woman in childbirth appears frequently (Isa. 13.8; 21.3; Jer. 4.31; 48.41), although detailed descriptions of actual births are lacking. The biblical writers knew and conveyed that childbirth was dangerous, however. In the eastern Mediterranean world during the Iron Age, only 1.9 children survived out of the average 4.1 births per female. The threat to women in the process of giving birth was also great, as most women before the nineteenth century CE died before reaching menopause, at about age 30 in the Iron Age (Angel 1972, 95). In ancient Israel, a woman had to become pregnant nearly twice for every child that survived to age five and women's lifespans were approximately ten years shorter than those of men, who are believed to have lived to age 40 on average (Meyers 1997, 28). "Burial statistics that show a high rate of infant mortality and short female life span explain ancient Near Eastern people's preoccupation with human fertility and child-stealing spirits" (Willett 2008, 97).

The reason why there are no lengthy descriptions of childbirth in the Hebrew Bible is because it is unlikely that many men, including the biblical writers, actually attended a birth; therefore, any information available from the biblical text is second hand. Jeremiah 20.14–15 suggests that men were not present at births: "Cursed be the day on which I was born! The day when my mother bore me, let it not be blessed! Cursed be the man who brought the news to my father, saying, 'A child is born to you, a son,' making him very glad." According to Palestinian ethnography, a man would leave the house when his wife was in labor. Her husband called for a midwife, the woman's female relatives and those of her husband came to help and her female neighbors gathered around her (Granqvist 1931, 56–58). One informant related that women had great interest in the event and all wanted to be present: "the mother and the mother-in-law of the confined woman, also her married sisters and the sisters of her husband, if married, ought to be there, especially if it is the first child. With the second and third it is not so important. A barren woman who wishes to have children also likes to be there. It is thought that in that way she will herself get children" (Granqvist 1931, 60). During childbirth, the women prayed and warded off any evil spirits that might be present (Granqvist 1947, 63).

The usual location of childbirth is in the woman's house, although some passages — such as the story of Rachel, who gave birth on the road — describe childbirth in less than ideal circumstances. Judging from the purity prescriptions related to menstruation and childbirth in the Hebrew Bible, it is possible that a specific room in the four-room house would have been used as a birthing room when the occasion arose. Since the four-room house could have accommodated the separation of women and men during periods of impurity, one of the rear rooms on the bottom floor, like the room used for the celebration of Orah's first menstruation (see Chapter 3), may have been the setting for childbirth and its aftermath. In Orah's husband's house, the rear space is a single broad room that is used by the women in the family for giving birth, menstruation and ritual activities. The ethnographic sources indicate that a woman might have been physically separated from the rest of her family by a wooden partition until her period of uncleanliness was over (Granqvist 1931, 116).

Specialized equipment seems to have been employed during childbirth in the form of a birth stool or, more likely, birth bricks. Exodus 1.16 mentions the birth stool or bricks — 'obnayim — as the surface upon which a newborn was placed after birth. Interestingly, the same word appears only one other time in the Hebrew Bible, in Jer. 18.3. In this passage the word 'obnayim refers to a potter's wheel or some other piece of pot making equipment, linking human reproduction to pottery production (McGeough 2006). Near Eastern and Egyptian textual sources indicate that birth bricks were commonly used as a squatting place for the woman giving birth. The first archaeological example of a birth brick was unearthed in a Middle Kingdom context at Abydos, in southern Egypt. The brick, which was found within a group of rooms in the mayor's house that seem to have been associated with the mayor's daughter, has a painted image of a seated woman holding a child; these figures are flanked by two female attendants. Two standards of the goddess Hathor, who was closely associated with fertility and childbirth in Egypt, are also in the scene. The brick's four edges were decorated with magical scenes, and any painted image original to the upper part of the brick is worn away, apparently through use (Wegner 2002, 3–4). The birth stool or bricks were ritually significant in ancient Near Eastern, Egyptian and Hittite birth ritual texts.

Women in Egypt and Palestine in the last century also gave birth in a squatting position. An Egyptian source describes the use of a confinement chair where women could give birth in a squatting position; if a chair was not available, a woman might squat while supporting herself on a large sieve stood on end (Blackman 1927, 63). In Palestine, women brought a stone into the house, put it on the floor, covered it with rags and spread dust from outside around it before the laboring woman squatted upon it (Granqvist 1931, 61–62). After the baby was born, the dust was taken out of the house with the afterbirth and buried so that no blood remained (Granqvist 1931, 97–98). There are two biblical passages that describe babies being born on the knees. In the story of Rachel (Gen. 30.3), this act represented a sort of adoption or acceptance of the baby — who was born to her husband Jacob and her maid Bilhah — by Rachel, while in the story of Joseph (Gen. 50.23), the birth of the third generation of his sons "on his knees" had a legal meaning related to land tenure (Gursky 2001, 81–82).

Several birth rituals are hinted at in the Hebrew Bible. Ezekiel 16.4 describes the actions to be taken immediately after a baby is delivered and the cord is cut: the baby is bathed, rubbed with salt and swaddled in cloth strips. Rubbing the baby with salt might have been a purification rite in response to the blood of childbirth (Gursky 2001, 85–94). Midwives still rubbed salt and oil on newborn babies before swaddling them in early twentieth-century Palestine (Granqvist 1931, 98; Grant 1907, 66). One witness reported that the midwife came back every day for seven days after the birth and rubbed the baby with salt and oil mixed together; it was believed that this was good for the skin of the child and had an effect on character (Granqvist 1931, 98). Rubbing salt on a newborn girl could also be a parallel ritual to male circumcision; both were purification rites that also served the purpose of invoking Yahweh's covenant and joining the baby into the community (Gursky 2001, 90).

Another birth ritual that might be related to rubbing salt on a newborn and male circumcision is naming (Gursky 2001, 93). Naming a newborn is more often than not a woman's prerogative; in the Hebrew Bible, mothers name their children 27 times, while fathers name their children 17 times (Meyers 1999a, note 27). Names in ancient Israel were more than just identification; they signified a person's essence and were thus extremely important (Meyers 2002b, 292). In the story of Ruth, the "women of the neighborhood" uniquely gave the newborn Obed his name (Ruth 4.17). This group of women came together in solidarity around the new mother, which would have been extremely important in a situation where a woman has only recently moved, alone, to her husband's village (Meyers 1999a, 120).

Symbolic objects may have been involved in reproductive rituals and childbirth as well. In the story of the birth of Tamar's twins in Genesis 38, Tamar's midwife ties a red thread around the firstborn baby's hand. In addition to serving as a marker of the first baby to appear, the red thread may have been an amulet. Biblical references to red thread (Exod. 25.4; 26.1; Lev. 14.4, 6, 49–52; Num. 4.8; Josh. 2.18) indicate that the color red symbolizes both blood and life (Gursky 2001, 64). The red thread might represent the newborn's life, especially in the situation of the unusually difficult birth of twins, or it may have had protective powers, since newborns in ancient Israel, Mesopotamia and Egypt wore cords or knotted bands to protect them from evil (Willett 1999, 334). Midwives might have carried red thread with them, or it may have been available in households generally (Gursky 2001, 66–67). Archaeological evidence and textual sources show that amulets and figurines were used in the ancient Near East and Egypt to protect newborn babies and new mothers; it is possible that these objects (see below) would have been carried by midwives for use during and immediately following childbirth as well. Red thread continued to have amuletic power among Sephardic women living in Jerusalem in the 1980s, and it was reported that women took red thread to Rachel's tomb in Bethlehem to "measure" the tomb, and wore the thread afterward as a charm (Sered 1992, 120).

All women apparently experienced a period of impurity following child-birth. According to Lev. 12.1-5, a woman underwent blood purification for 40 days if she had borne a son and 70 days if she had borne a daughter.[1] There are various explanations for why a woman would experience a longer period of impurity after giving birth to a girl; it might be that the shorter period of impurity for a boy implies that boys are better than girls (Stol 2000, 207), or it could be that male circumcision purified the mother indirectly, shortening the length of her postpartum period of impurity (Gursky 2001, 90). The eighth day after birth is the day when a newborn male should be cir-cumcised according to Lev. 12.3; immediately following this commandment the text reads: "Her [the postpartum woman] time of blood purification shall be thirty-three days; she shall not touch any holy thing, or come into the sanctuary, until the days of her purification are completed" (Lev. 12.4). Postpartum bleeding can last up to six weeks, which accords well with the minimum period of impurity in Lev. 12.4.

The Hebrew Bible says nothing about the handling of the afterbirth, but sources from twentieth-century Palestine and Egypt indicate that it had magical properties and needed to be treated carefully. In Palestine, the dust from around the birthing stone is taken outside along with the afterbirth and buried deep in the earth (Granqvist 1931, 97–98). In Egypt, if a woman is anxious about having another child, she buries the afterbirth under the threshold to her house; when she steps over it three, five or seven times its spirit will reenter her body and be born again as another child (Blackman 1927, 63). In some circumstances, the afterbirth is preserved for use in ritu-als to protect the house. According to a Palestinian informant, one family preserved the afterbirth in a jar and put it beside the door inside the house to frighten away *Karinah*, a spirit that was believed to threaten babies (Granqvist

1931, 97). In our story, Orah's midwife buries the placenta under the entrance to the rear room the night of the birth to provide protection for Orah and her newborn son.

Amulets and Jewelry

Amulets and jewelry were important possessions of both women and men in ancient Israel. Jewelry was used in a variety of ways: it could serve as a sign of wealth and status, a form of currency, for religious purposes and, of course, as adornment (King and Stager 2001, 276). Amulets — which are essentially charms believed to protect people as well as places from perceived harm — were especially important for women who wanted to avoid the potential dangers associated with conception, childbirth and infancy, since these were times when the use of amulets for their potent apotropaic — or protective — powers were most vital. There was a widespread belief in the ancient Near East and Egypt that demons and other dark forces threatened pregnant women and children; in ancient Israel, women used a variety of protective objects to deflect jealous child-stealing demons and the evil eye from harming themselves and their children.

Individual pieces of jewelry are mentioned frequently in the Hebrew Bible, and the abundant archaeological remains and iconographic sources permit us insight into their technology, appearance and function. The most detailed list of jewelry is found in Isa. 3.18-23, which is a catalogue of jewelry and clothing items owned by the women of Jerusalem. Some of the jewelry terms are obscure, although correlating the archaeological remains of jewelry to the terms on the list allows for a secure identification of most of them; among the items on this list are anklets, pendants, beads, crowns, signet rings and nose rings (Platt 1992, 830–32). Wedding jewelry is described in Gen. 24.22, 53 and Ezek. 16.11-12. Evidence that jewelry was worn by both women and men in ancient Israel is demonstrated not only by the biblical accounts, but also archaeologically: jewelry is so common in Iron Age burials that practically all of them contain beads, anklets, bracelets or earrings (King and Stager 2001, 277).

Metal plaques, inscribed gems and other jewelry items were in widespread use in the ancient Near East for protection and divine blessing. In the Hebrew Bible, examples of amulets include texts of Yahweh's deeds or commands inscribed on bands (Exod. 13.9, 16; Deut. 6.8; 11.18), tablets worn as jewelry (Exod. 35.22; Num. 31.50) and the high priest Aaron's breastplate with its 12 engraved gemstones (Exod. 28.17-21). The best-known archaeological examples of Iron Age amulets, discovered in a tomb at Ketef Hinnom, in Jerusalem, are two small silver scrolls that were inscribed before being rolled up and worn as necklaces on a cord or chain. Dating to approximately 600 BCE, the scrolls are incised with the Priestly Benediction in Num. 6:24-26, making them the earliest-known occurrences of a text from the Hebrew Bible. The apparent function of these amulets was to invoke Yahweh's divine protection against evil (Barkay, *et al.* 2004, 68). It is impossible to know whether these amulets were used in life or intended only as funerary offerings; unfortunately, it also cannot be known if these amulets were originally deposited with females or males in this large burial cave.

Various other jewelry items used as amulets have been found in ancient Israel, including Egyptian-style scarabs, scaraboids and iconic seals. Scarabs are small, beetle-shaped objects that were made from a variety of materials; scaraboids were derived from scarabs but depict different animals. Seals assumed many different shapes and were incised with various motifs, and could serve as a form of wealth storage depending on the expense of the material used. They could be used for administrative purposes as a way of signing documents, they could be status symbols or they could be used as amulets (Limmer 2007). In addition, Egyptian-style amulets in the form of three-dimensional sculpture were used in Egypt for good luck and protection, and it is likely that they served similar functions in ancient Israel, where they were imported. Small figurines of the Egyptian dwarf god Bes like the one in Figure 5.2 from Iron II Ashkelon, in particular, may have been used to protect women and their babies during childbirth (Willett 1999, 310). Although many Bes amulets were imported from Egypt, molds for making Bes figurines have been found in Iron II sites in Palestine, attesting to local production (Meyers 2002b, 287). Protective amulets worn by children around the neck are mentioned in Prov. 6.21-22, although we do not know what form these amulets took.

Nearly all of these Egyptian or Egyptian-style amulets were made of faience, a sort of pre-glass, in a blue-green color that was probably not coincidental (Limmer 2007, 386), since the color blue protects against the evil eye. Other objects that functioned as amulets in ancient Israel were beads, including eye beads, and divine eye designs on women's accessories, like stone cosmetic palettes and ivory palettes (Willett 1999, 312–20). The modern concept of the evil eye in the Middle East and eastern Mediterranean has its origins in the ancient Near East and Egypt, and the idea of a jealous evil eye is seen in the Hebrew Bible in 1 Sam. 18.9, when Saul "eyed David" and attempted to kill him after he was seized by an evil spirit.

There are abundant ethnographic examples of the continued use of protective amulets in twentieth-century Palestine. Many of these amulets were

5.2 Bes amulet (after King and Stager 2001, Ill. 152).

intended to protect the wearer from the evil eye, which was brought on by the look of a jealous person with or without an evil intent (Limmer 2007, 37–40). Various blue items — including beads and glass bracelets — were hung over the door to a newly built home to protect it from the harmful effects of the evil eye and the *Karinah* (Canaan 1933, 63; Grant 1907, 116). Blue beads were sewn onto the cloth caps worn by infants and children to protect them from the evil eye (Grant 1907, 67), and blue eye pendants and hand charms were worn around the necks of children and animals for protection (Wilson 1906, 49). Even blue tattoos on the face were believed to avert the evil eye (Grant 1907, 117). Amulets and other blue items continue to be powerful protection against evil forces in the eastern Mediterranean world today.

A study of the archaeological contexts of amulets in eighth-century BCE Lachish revealed that figurines and jewelry are found in the same contexts as weaving and cooking implements in houses, demonstrating the importance of magic jewelry and female figurines in the everyday lives of women in the Iron Age II (Willett 1999, 335–39). Similar patterns are seen in the artifact assemblages excavated from houses at Iron Age II Tel el-Farah (north), Beersheba, Tell Halif and other sites (Willett 2008, 91–93). Unfortunately, relatively few jewelry items have been uncovered in Iron Age I contexts, and there are probably several reasons for this disparity.[2] Regardless of the reason, we know less about jewelry from the period under discussion than from the subsequent Iron Age II, although it is likely that jewelry and amulets of various types were in use in the highland villages.

In our story Orah wears an eye pendant around her neck to protect her from evil forces during her pregnancy, and the Astarte figurine in the rear room where she gives birth also functions as an amulet to protect her and her newborn during and immediately following the birth. When her baby is born, a string of blue beads is tied around his neck as well; these amulets, along with the rituals performed by the midwife and the prayers and chants of the women during and after the birth, serve as defense against the dark forces believed to threaten the postpartum woman and her newborn child.

Basketry

Related to textile production (see Chapter 2), basket weaving was an essential craft in ancient Israel about which we know relatively little because it leaves few traces. Baskets include those "[o]bjects made of plant parts of limited length often with a shape specific to the particular plant part" (Wendrich 2000, 254). The division between textiles and basketry is somewhat arbitrary, although the basket maker has to deal with the irregular shape of raw materials and short strands she or he is working with, unlike the weaver, who uses thread of uniform size along the entire length (Wendrich 2000, 254). Based on ethnographic, biblical and archaeological sources from Egypt, we can assume that baskets and various other types of woven containers, mats and other items were made primarily by women for household use in ancient Israel. In our story, Orah places her baby in a cradle that she has woven specifically for this purpose in the final weeks of her pregnancy, and she sleeps next to it on a woven mat on the floor. Woven objects are used for a variety of purposes in Orah's house, and she and the other women in her household make them from straw, grass and other locally available materials.

Baskets are often described as containers for food in the Hebrew Bible. In Gen. 40.16-18, as Joseph recounts his dreams to Pharaoh, the three baskets of bread on Joseph's head that were eaten by birds represent three days. Baskets as containers for bread are also mentioned in various other passages (Exod. 29.3, 23, 32; Lev. 8.2, 26, 31; Num. 6.15, 17, 19), and baskets are also containers for grapes (Deut. 23.24; 26.2), meat (Judg. 6.19), figs (Jer. 24.2), and more. The use of baskets as tools — like sieves used to separate wheat from chaff — is mentioned in Isa. 30.28; such tools might have been used by women on a daily basis as they made bread and other foods from cereal grains (see Chapter 2).

Most closely related to the subject of childbirth is the reference to Moses' basket in Exodus 2. In this passage, Moses' mother Jochabed takes a papyrus basket coated with tar and pitch, places Moses inside it and casts it on the Nile in an effort to save the child. In Exod. 2.5-6, Pharaoh's daughter sees the basket and sends her maid to open it; when she does, the crying child, which Pharaoh's daughter recognizes as a Hebrew, is revealed. Although no other biblical passage specifically mentions the use of baskets as cradles or carriers for children, ethnographic information suggests that woven textiles and baskets were commonly used for such purposes.

Little physical evidence for basketry exists from ancient Israel because the climate in this region does not usually preserve organic material. Only a few pieces of Iron Age basketry have been excavated, including two sieves made of unspun plant fibers found at Kuntillat 'Ajrud (Sheffer and Tidhar 1991, 11–12). The impressions of woven mats on the bottoms of ceramic vessels — which formed before the clay had thoroughly dried — also provide some information about ancient basketry. We have much more evidence from neighboring Egypt, where conditions of preservation are very good; woven objects found there, especially in tombs, include baskets, bags, mats, sieves, pot stands, nets, brushes, brooms, boxes, coffins, furniture and sandals (Wendrich 2000, 254). We can imagine that many of the same objects were used in ancient Israel as well.

Photographs from late-nineteenth–early twentieth-century Palestine show women making baskets and mats, and provide firsthand evidence for the use of baskets in numerous daily-life activities.[3] Women wove baskets from straw and other materials and dyed them various colors. Sieves were used to clean grain, and baskets were used by women and men to gather produce from the fields and carry various items on the head. Straw mats often covered the dirt floors of houses, and women made large round trays that were used as serving dishes for bread, grapes, figs and other foods. Babies were sometimes carried by women in baskets on their heads, and one source described a baby swaddled and sleeping on a circular woven mat that was placed on a shallow straw basket of the kind used to carry wheat.

One description of basket making in a twentieth-century Palestinian village provides information about the technology and physical context of this activity: "[a]fter the wheat had been threshed, women selected the longer, unbroken stalks for basket making, an activity reserved for winter when there was little work to be done in the fields. Women often sat around the fireplace, working their straw objects with rhythm and great artistry, and produced a colorful range of functional and luxury containers and trays" (Amiry and Tamari 1989, 42). These observers also describe how women soaked the stalks in tubs before they could be woven, and the process of dyeing the stalks red, green, purple and orange.

In our story, Orah's newborn son sleeps in a basket that would have protected him from the beaten earth floor and provided extra warmth in the cool evenings. Baskets are also used to collect the last of the summer fruit for transport back to the household. Like spinning thread, weaving baskets was an activity carried out by women when their hands were not occupied with other work; also like spinning, the rhythmic work of weaving baskets was a relaxing activity that could be done with other women and while caring for young children. For Orah, it is an activity that provides some pleasure during the final, long days of her pregnancy as she anxiously prepares for the birth of her first child.

For Further Reading

Gursky, M.D. 2001. *Reproductive Rituals in Biblical Israel*. Unpublished Ph.D. Dissertation, New York University. An analysis of the belief and ritual system underlying reproduction in ancient Israel according to the Hebrew Bible and other Near Eastern textual sources.

Stol, M. 2000. *Birth in Babylonia and the Bible: Its Mediterranean Setting*. Cuneiform Monographs 14. Groningen: Styx Publications. A comprehensive analysis of birth in biblical and ancient Near Eastern texts that follows mother and child from conception to weaning. Includes a detailed discussion of the demons that were believed to threaten young children and their mothers, and the amulets and other magical items that were used for protection.

Willett, E.A.R. 2008. Infant Mortality and Women's Religion in the

Biblical Periods. In *The World of Women in the Ancient and Classical Near East*, ed. B.A. Nakhai, 79–98. Newcastle upon Tyne: Cambridge Scholars. Discusses the household as the center for women's religious activities related to the protection of children from child-stealing demons. Analysis of the archaeological remains from Iron Age houses shows that amulets and protective figurines are found alongside artifacts related to food preparation and textile production, demonstrating that these protective items were used by women.

Notes

1 Since much of Leviticus is assigned to the Priestly tradition, which many scholars believe to be exilic, the purity regulations in Leviticus may not be applicable to highland village life in the early Iron Age.

2 Iron Age II jewelry is frequently found in burials and many fewer Iron Age I tombs than Iron II tombs have been excavated (Bloch-Smith 2004). We might expect that metal jewelry items, like anklets, bangles, earrings and nose rings, were less common in the early Iron Age because of the relative poverty of the central highland villages compared to the Iron Age II cities that have yielded the largest amounts of jewelry and jewelry elements. It is also possible that some of the jewelry, particularly elements made of organic or recyclable materials (like metals), did not survive.

3 See Grant 1907, 66, 76, 92, 256 and photos pp. 38, 48, 150, 230; Graham-Brown 1980, Chapter 1, photo 40, Chapter 4, photo 6, and Chapter 5, photo 4; Vamosh 2008, photo p. 43.

Chapter 6
Motherhood

Orah had not participated in the annual pilgrimage to the shrine at Shiloh in some years, having chosen instead to stay behind in the village to care for her two young children. Her son, now age eight, is old enough to accompany her husband and other family members on the trip without her, but Orah had just recently weaned her three-year-old daughter Hilah, and now felt ready to make the long trip on foot with both of her children. Orah was sad that it had come time to wean what would probably be her last child, but she looked forward to the opportunity to offer thanks to Yahweh for her fertility at his shrine in Shiloh and celebrate the weaning with her sister Adah. Orah and Adah lived in villages located several hours' walk apart, and Orah had never visited her sister's village; the annual pilgrimage to Shiloh was the only time Orah could plan to see her older sister and other relatives from her birth village, and she had missed them greatly the past few years.

The pilgrimage coincided with the end of the olive harvest season, and the trip would give the members of Orah's household a chance to offer thanks for a successful crop and take a break from the last major harvest of the agricultural year. The olive harvest had begun several weeks earlier, as the olives began to ripen on the silvery trees on the terraces surrounding the village; all members of Orah's household participated in the harvest, including the young children, who were allowed to rest or play in the groves when they tired of collecting olives from the ground in their own small baskets. Orah and the other women in her household would press the olives using mortars and pestles, and then store the oil in jars for use in cooking, protecting the skin and lighting the clay lamps in the evenings. Because of their value, Orah's brother-in-law, his wife and their children would remain behind to guard the olive groves while the rest of the household went on the pilgrimage this year.

Orah had begun making preparations for the trip several weeks ahead of time. When she could spare an hour or two away from the olive groves, she worked on the skins from the two goats that had been slaughtered for the feast of *'asip* only a few weeks before. Hilah stayed at her mother's side as Orah soaked the skins in a large ceramic basin in the courtyard, and the little girl was allowed to help with the tanning by throwing rinds from the pomegranates they had been collecting since the summer harvest into the basin. Orah intended to donate them to the priests at Shiloh since she knew that fine skins and leather were required for the Tabernacle at the shrine, and she hoped that her contribution would be used for such honorable purposes. She also made several new skin bags to store the family's food and drink for the trip; now that her children were getting older, they needed to carry enough to sustain them in case there was not enough food or water available for the pilgrims at Shiloh.

In addition to the hides she was making for the Tabernacle and the food and drink she was preparing for her family, Orah organized several other offerings for the shrine, including a juglet of fine oil from the first olive pressing of the season and a small sack of flour ground from the barley stored since the spring harvest. Along with the bedding and goat hair covers for the tents, she would pack the sacks of food and skins of water on the back of the family's donkey, which would accompany them on the trip for this purpose. Large crowds came to Shiloh for the annual feast, and Orah's family would set up camp along with hundreds of others on the outskirts of the village for the duration of the event. She hoped to find Adah's family quickly so they could set up their tents together.

When the day came to leave, the family ate the morning meal and began walking as soon as the sun rose. As they walked through the olive groves, they said a quick goodbye to Orah's brother-in-law, who had slept under the temporary shelter the night before, and they promised to ask Yahweh to bless him for staying behind so the rest of the family could attend the festival. Hilah was excited to travel so far from her village and she walked alongside the donkey for the first hour or so, slowing the group as she stopped to examine the wildflowers and lizards she saw darting through the rocks. As she began to tire, Orah slung the child on her back in a woven sling and carried her awhile so she could rest. As midday approached, the group stopped to eat some of the preserved cheese and parched grain that Orah had prepared the day before, and by early afternoon the road became more crowded as other groups much like Orah's slowly made their way to Shiloh. Orah and her husband talked about the time they had first seen each other on this road years before, and Orah offered a silent prayer of thanks to her deceased parents for choosing this man as her husband.

When Orah finally saw the town in the distance she pointed it out to Hilah, who was now sitting on the pile of bedding on the donkey; in the late afternoon sun the place was teeming with life as hundreds, even thousands, of people converged on the site, staking their tents on the village outskirts. Although Orah would not find Adah and her family until the next day, she was glad to finally make camp and chat with the women in the closely packed tents around hers. She told them of her daughter's weaning, and invited them to celebrate with her family in the days ahead; the women offered to say a special blessing at the shrine to honor this important occasion. As the sky darkened and the hearths built outside the tents were lit for the evening, Orah put her little daughter to sleep and lay down herself, tired from the long trip. Her husband and son entered the village to learn of the plans for the upcoming days of the festival, and they returned after dark with the news that a feast would be held the following evening and the family would be able to visit the shrine itself in the next day or two. Orah said a prayer to Yahweh thanking him for the blessing of her family before she drifted off to sleep, comforted by the murmuring of a hundred voices around her.

Introduction

Motherhood was one of the most important roles that a woman could play in ancient Israel; indeed, "[a] woman's influence was greatest as a mother" (Marsman 2003, 242). Motherhood is used metaphorically in the Hebrew Bible as an honorable position, such as when Deborah is called "a mother in Israel" (Judg. 5.7). A child is to honor both father and mother according to the Fifth Commandment in Exod. 20.12, and women were largely responsible for educating and socializing young children (Chapter 2). As discussed in Chapter 5, having children was a woman's highest priority in ancient Israel, and having children was essential for agricultural success in the Iron I villages. In our story, Orah, who is 26 years old with two surviving children, has just weaned her young daughter and is preparing to celebrate this important event at the annual pilgrimage to Shiloh.

Children were a universal concern of all women in the Hebrew Bible, and there are many expressions of a mother's emotion for her children. The special feeling of a mother for her son in particular is a common expression (Bird 1997, 34), but there are many other examples of women weeping over (Jer. 31.15), worrying about (Judg. 5.28-30) and otherwise showing strong feelings for their children (2 Kgs 4.18-20). Mothers sometimes chose to give up their children in order to save their lives, such as when Jochabed sends her son Moses down the Nile in a basket (Exod. 2.3) and when the true mother saves her child from Solomon's judgment to divide the boy in half (1 Kgs 3.16-28). Women are also depicted loving their adult sons, such as when Saul's concubine Rizpah kept vigil over the bodies of her slain sons until they were given a proper burial (2 Sam. 21.10) (Marsman 2003, 237–38).

Since few women survived to menopause and young women began having children soon after puberty, as much as one-third of a woman's lifespan might include the physical processes of motherhood, including pregnancy, breastfeeding and taking care of young children (Meyers 1997, 28). Since women were primarily responsible for the care of young children, the efforts of childrearing must have been compatible with women's productive labor. Although many daily-life activities were carried out in the house and courtyard, as we have seen, women also spent considerable time beyond the family compound. Women may have sometimes left their young children in the care of older children or elderly members of the household, but during the busy harvest seasons, when every member of the community was needed in the fields and agricultural terraces, young children accompanied their mothers. Breastfeeding infants were certainly physically close to their mothers much of the time.

Although the biblical writers do not describe how small children were carried by their mothers, the ethnographic sources describe women carrying their children in various ways. In twentieth-century CE Palestine, children were worn in woven slings suspended down the mother's back and supported by a strap worn across the woman's forehead. Photographs and firsthand accounts also document these slings being hung on pegs or in trees so that small babies could sleep while their mothers worked nearby.[1] Women might also carry their children in baskets on the head or on one shoulder (Granqvist 1981, plate 34). An Iron Age II pillar figurine from Tell Beit Mirsim depicts a woman carrying a child on her back with the child's hands wrapped around her neck (Keel and Uehlinger 1998, figure 326). In our story, Orah carries her young daughter in a woven sling part of the way to Shiloh and allows her to sit on the overloaded donkey as well. Hilah is used to being physically close to her mother nearly all of the time, and only now, at the age of weaning, is she beginning to discover her independence.

Breastfeeding and Weaning

There are many ancient sources that suggest that children were breastfed for two or three years and the same is true in the modern Middle East (Stol 2000, 181). Nursing one's children would have been an important aspect of female childrearing, and only in the case of maternal death or insufficient milk supply would family members assist in feeding a newborn (Gruber 2000b, 277). Women in ancient Israel are also believed to have nursed their children for at least two to three years, and this may have contributed to the relatively low fertility of ancient Israelite women (Gruber 1989, 63). Ethnographic research of contemporary societies has shown that prolonged nursing delays ovulation and allows for birth spacing; prolonged nursing helped ensure that a mother would not have to wean a child early if she quickly became pregnant with another. This might be apparent in Hos. 1.8, which reads: "When she [Gomer] had weaned Lo-Ruhamah, she conceived and bore a son" (Gruber 1989, 68). Nursing also promotes bonding between mothers and their infants, which is expressed in the artistic images of suckling babies from the ancient Near East and Egypt and the close relationships that developed between individuals and their wet nurses described in the ancient texts (see below).

There are two biblical passages that mention women nursing their own children: Sarah in Gen. 21.7-8 and Hannah in 1 Sam. 1.22-24. Sarah nurses her son Isaac for an undefined length of time, and we learn in Gen. 21.8 that his weaning was marked with a celebration. After Hannah's son Samuel is born through Yahweh's intervention, she does not attend the annual sacrifice at Shiloh until the baby is weaned. Hannah's husband Elkanah finds this acceptable, saying: "Do what seems best to you, wait until you have weaned him" (1 Sam. 1.23). This passage may demonstrate that nursing a baby took precedence over cultic obligations (Gruber 1989, 67). Although it is unclear how long Hannah nursed Samuel, we can assume it was at least several years.

The age of weaning in Palestine in the early twentieth century was variable. According to one source, a boy was nursed for two-and-a-half years and a girl for one-and-a-half years; it was believed to be dangerous to pamper a girl, but the longer a boy is nursed, the better (Granqvist 1931, 108). It has been suggested that weaning a girl earlier would have allowed a woman in ancient Israel to try again for a son sooner (Gruber 1989, 68). According to another ethnographic source, children were nursed for an average of two years, but a woman's last child might be weaned only at age four or five (Grant 1907, 66). In traditional societies where infant mortality rates are high, extended nursing is healthier for children, especially in cases where food is scarce.

There was a widespread belief in the ancient Near East that the suckling infant was threatened, and women used amulets to protect their milk supply from evil influences (Willett 1999, 372). Female figurines with large breasts might have been used to protect a woman's milk supply from forces that attempted to drain them and substitute poison for milk (Willett 1999, 372–73). Although breast amulets from the early Iron Age have not been identified, the Judean pillar figurines (see Figure 6.1) common in the eighth–sixth centuries BCE may have been used by women to protect themselves and their children (Willett 1999, 382), and perhaps a woman's ability to nurse. Most of these figurines represent females with large breasts and tapering bodies resembling tree trunks, and some have suggested that these are images of the goddess Asherah. One example from Tell Beit Mirsim shows a woman

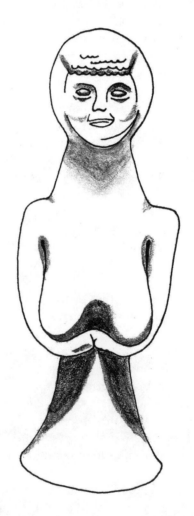

6.1 Pillar figurine (after King and Stager 2001, Ill. 218).

carrying a child on her back, suggesting that the female form depicted is a nursing mother (Keel and Uehlinger 1998, 333), and several fragmentary examples from Jerusalem may depict females cradling infants in their arms (Byrne 2004, 142 [figure]), showing, perhaps, that these are images of real women engaged in activities related to childcare.[2]

Interestingly, the only biblical narrative that describes a wet nurse in some detail (Exod. 2.9) is also the only passage that talks about the growth of the Hebrew population in Egypt (Exod. 1.7, 20). In this passage, Moses' mother Jochabed is paid by Pharaoh's daughter to nurse her own son. There are several other biblical references to wet nurses, however. The bond that can develop between a wet nurse and a child is seen in Gen. 24.59 and 35.8, which describe Rebekah's nurse, Deborah. Deborah was apparently close to Rebekah throughout her life, and when Deborah died she was buried under an oak tree below Bethel which was named the "Oak of Weeping" (Gen. 35.8). In addition, Joash was hidden in the Temple with his wet nurse while the queen mother, Athaliah, killed his family in an attempt to hold royal power after her son, King Ahaziah, was assassinated (2 Kgs 11.2-3). The stories of Joash and Moses' nurses are rare examples of the employment of wet nurses by privileged families in ancient Israel.

There is much textual evidence from the ancient Near East and Egypt for professional wet nurses, who were usually women of the lower classes or slaves hired for several years. These texts report that strong bonds developed between wet nurses and suckling infants (Stol 2000), such as in the case of Rebekah and her nurse Deborah. Employing a wet nurse might have been a strategy of affluent women to maximize their fertility (Gruber 2000b, 277) since weaning would allow a woman to get pregnant more quickly and increase the size of her family. In Iron I Israel, wet nurses were probably not employed unless required because of the death of the mother or insufficient milk supply. Even when wet nurses were employed, mothers were still largely responsible for educating and socializing their young children.

Weaning was an important event because it meant that a child had survived to age two or three. It was apparently an occasion for celebration, such as when Sarah and Abraham's son Isaac's weaning is "marked by a festive party" (Gruber 1989, 68) in Gen. 21.8. Isaiah 28.9-10 suggests that children were even older than age two or three when they were weaned; some may have continued to nurse when they could first learn to distinguish letters.[3] In our story, Orah's family celebrates the weaning of Hilah at Shiloh; at three years old, she has survived the dangerous period of infancy and early childhood.

Olive Harvest and Olive Oil Production

Olives were one of the most important crops grown in the region in antiquity, and the importance of olive trees is suggested by Deut. 8.8, where they are listed as one of the seven most important crops and fruit trees in the land. Olive trees are native to Palestine and archaeological evidence suggests that the trees' most valuable product — olive oil — was extracted from the olive fruit in prehistoric times, at least from the Chalcolithic period (c. 4500–3200 BCE) at sites in the Golan Heights (Epstein 1993). In ancient Israel, planting olive trees was an investment in the future, since it takes years for an olive tree to mature enough to produce fruit; thus, it would have been important for the highland settlers to plant olive trees soon after their arrival to provide for future generations. The trees do particularly well in the rocky, shallow soils found on the highland terraces, and do not need to compete with cereal crops for more fertile soil. The olive groves owned by Orah's husband's family are located on the terraces just outside the village.

Olives ripen in September or October, and the Feast of Ingathering — *'asip/sukkot* — may have coincided with this period, as "ingathering" may refer here to the harvest of this late fruit. In Exod. 34.22, the Feast of Ingathering is observed at the "turn of the year," while in Exod. 23.16 it is at the end of the agricultural year, which is presumably the end of the fall harvest (Vanderkam 1992, 817). The harvest period would have been one of hard work and celebration among the highland villagers, and women participated along with other family members in both the olive harvest and oil pressing for their households.

Biblical references to the actual consumption of olives and olive oil are lacking. Leviticus 6.14-15 describes a grain offering cooked with oil on a griddle, but olive oil is not specified and the offering was intended for Yahweh, not for actual human consumption. There are many more references to other uses of olive oil in sacred contexts: it was used to light lamps in the Tabernacle and, later, in the Jerusalem Temple (Exod. 25.6; 35.14; 39.37), and olive oil was required to anoint prophets, kings and priests (Exod. 28.41, Judg. 9.8; 1 Kgs 19.16).[4] Olive wood was used to construct the cherubim and various architectural features in the Jerusalem Temple (1 Kgs 6.23; 31-33). Olive oil and other products of the olive tree were used in many secular, everyday activities as well (see below).

The biblical writers do not offer much about the olive harvest or the technology of olive oil processing, but relevant information can be learned from ethnographic accounts from twentieth-century Palestine and the archaeological remains. According to one source, "olives and olive oil were, and still are, the most valuable produce of the Palestinian countryside, and most village fields contained olive groves. The olive-picking season, which lasted between two and four weeks . . . began in late October or early November" (Amiry and Tamari 1989, 35). Details about the harvest provide insights into ancient harvesting methods as well: "[e]arly in the morning on the specified day, all the inhabitants of the village went to the olive groves with their mules and donkeys loaded with ladders, baskets, sacks, long sticks and food. Once there the men spread sheets on the ground beneath the trees, climbed the trees or a ladder, and shook the olives down onto the sheets. Alternatively, the branches were beaten with long sticks. Women and children then put the olives in straw baskets which were emptied into large sacks" (Amiry and Tamari 1989, 36). Other ethnographic sources confirm that women pick olives using baskets,[5] and beating olives from the trees, presumably with sticks, is referred to in Deut. 24.20 and Isa. 17.6; 24.13.

After the olives were transported back to the village, they could be treated in two ways: the oil could be expressed, or the olives could be preserved in water or brine until they were edible. There is no evidence that the ancient Israelites ate preserved olives, however, and it is likely that olive oil was the primary food product of the olive. Olive oil processing basically requires three steps: olives must be crushed to remove the pits; the olive meat and skins must be pressed to extract the oil; and the oil must be separated from water and other remains (Curtis 2001, 187). Olives were probably pressed several times to extract as much oil as possible, but the quality of the oil deteriorates with each subsequent pressing. The fine quality of oil from the first pressing — the virgin oil — was required for lighting lamps in the Jerusalem Temple and for the cereal offering to Yahweh (Exod. 27.20; 29.40; Num. 28.5) (Stager 1983, 242–43).

Ethnographic sources confirm that small amounts of olive oil can be expressed using a stone roller or mortar and pestle, which is pressing on a much smaller scale than seen in the Iron Age II, when sophisticated lever-and-weight presses were used in industrial olive processing and olive oil was exported throughout the Near East (Curtis 2001, 228). Given the dearth of olive presses at early Iron Age sites, it is likely that olive oil was expressed for household use with mortars, pestles and other equipment made of stone and wood during this period, and women were likely responsible for this household activity.[6]

As discussed in Chapter 3, olive oil was used as a base for various skin preparations and perfumes (Deut. 28.40; Isa. 1.6), and served as a moisturizer in the hot, dry climate. The many clay oil lamps found in archaeological excavations attest to the use of olive oil — the most widely available oil in ancient Israel — as a light source in domestic and other contexts. Olive oil was likely consumed in raw and cooked dishes, and bread was probably dipped in oil to provide extra flavor and calories. Olive pits were used to fuel ovens and kilns, and the remains from the second or third olive pressings could have been used to feed animals.[7] Orah and the other women in her household process ripe olives using stone mortars and pestles, and the resulting oil is used for various everyday purposes. Orah prepares some of the fine oil from the initial pressing as a donation for the shrine at Shiloh as well. We can imagine that the olive pits and other remains were not wasted, and were probably used as fuel for the ovens and fodder for the family's donkey, cattle and small flock of goats and sheep.

Hide Working

Although there are a number of biblical references to the use of animal skins as containers, coverings and clothing items, there is no information about the process of hide working preserved in the Hebrew Bible. Although industrial hide workers — or tanners — in the Iron Age II probably worked beyond the boundary of their towns and cities because of the smell (King and Stager 2001, 163), processing hides for household use in the Iron Age I was likely undertaken by women somewhere in or near their household compounds. Since organic material rarely survives, we have very few examples of items made from hides and skins from this period, but we can learn much from the many objects made of skins and hides that have survived from neighboring Egypt.

The Hebrew Bible provides some information about the use of skins and hides in sacred and secular contexts. Several skins were required in the construction of the Tabernacle; the outermost curtain or cover was apparently made of dolphin skin with a layer of ram's skin dyed red underneath (Exod. 26.14).[8] When the Tabernacle was to be moved, skin and leather coverings were used to cover Tabernacle accessories and holy things (Num. 4.6-25). The use of skin bags as containers is attested in numerous passages, such as when Hagar and Ishmael are sent away with bread and a water skin as their provisions (Gen. 21.14-15, 19) and when Jael offers Sisera milk from a skin when he enters her tent (Judg. 4.19). Hannah takes a skin full of wine and other offerings to the temple at Shiloh (1 Sam. 1.24), and skins are described as containers for wine in other passages (1 Sam. 10.3; 16.20; 2 Sam. 16.1). Leather was also used to make various clothing items, like shoes, belts (2 Kgs 1.8) and sandals (Ezek. 16.10). Other biblical uses of leather include David's sling (1 Sam. 17.40, 49-50) and horse saddles (Lev. 15.9).

The main concern of the tanner, then as today, is the preservation of the corium, which is the middle portion of the skin between the outer layer — the epidermis — and the under layer of adipose tissue. The corium has a fibrous structure which is known as the "grain" of the leather. The outer and inner layers must be removed through various mechanical and chemical processes before the corium can be treated with tanning agents to render it imputrescible (resistant to decay) and water resistant (Forbes 1966, 1–3). Ancient Egyptian tomb paintings depict some of the stages in ancient hide and skin processing as well as the tools that were used during the process (van Driel-Murray 2000, 302).

In the most basic of hide-working practices, sharp blades are used to remove the outer and inner layers and large containers are required for soaking hides and skins in water and other substances. Hides (referring to the pelts of larger animals) and skins (those from smaller animals) can then be treated in various ways depending on intended use. Vegetable tanning, the only permanent tanning process, was accomplished using infusions of tannic acid from the bark, pods and galls of certain trees and the rinds of pomegranates (Forbes 1966, 39). Sandals and other clothing articles, thongs used as ties and fasteners, bags and many other objects made of animal hides and skins have been preserved from ancient Egypt, and we can assume that some of the same items were made and used in ancient Israel as well.[9]

In Murdock and Provost's classic study of the division of labor by sex in traditional societies, manufacturing leather products ranked 29 and the preparation of skins ranked 26 out of 50 (the most female activity ranked 50), making these activities marginally more female associated than male associated (Murdock and Provost 1973, table 1). More recent ethnographic studies have shed light on the social aspects of hide working in traditional societies around the world; these have shown that the hide-working process is highly gendered, with specific activities, tools, spatial locations and other responsibilities allocated to either women or men. In many cases, women are indeed the primary hide workers, although men might also be involved in the manufacture and distribution of this valuable commodity (Frink and Weedman 2005).

Hide working, like food preparation, pottery production, spinning and weaving and basket making, was an important technology carried out in the household context in antiquity that was compatible with childcare. Hide working requires specialized skills, but not specialized tools; flint blades are still used to scrape hides in traditional societies, and it is possible that some of the flint tools found at Iron Age I sites were used in this way as well. Tanning materials, like the pomegranate rinds used in this story, are available locally, and the ceramic basin used to soak the skins could have been used in many other daily-life activities as well. Hilah assists Orah with the tanning of the goat skins, and this is part of the training she receives in various household crafts and technologies that will be important in her future.

Pilgrimage to Shiloh

In our story, Orah travels with her husband and children for an annual festival at Shiloh. Located in the highlands midway between Jerusalem and Shechem, Shiloh was less than a day's walk from Orah's husband's village. Shiloh was the religious capital of Israel until the Jerusalem Temple was built in the tenth century BCE, and Israel's holiest object — the Ark of the Covenant — resided in the Tabernacle at Shiloh until it was taken by the Philistines and the site destroyed. We do not know exactly when the annual feast at Shiloh occurred, and it may have been separate from the three prescribed feasts of *massot/pessah*, *shevuot* and *'asip/sukkot* (see Chapter 1). Some believe that the feast was part of an annual wine festival because, according to Judg. 21.19-21, the men of the tribe of Benjamin lay in wait in vineyards when the local girls came out to dance at Shiloh, but Menaham Haran notes that the girls danced in the vicinity of the shrine or on the outskirts of the settlement, not specifically in the vineyards (Haran 1977, 299). In our story, the pilgrimage to Shiloh takes place just after *'asip/sukkot* in early fall, during the olive harvest.

The site of Shiloh has been excavated in recent years by a team from Tel Aviv University, and archaeological remains dating to the Bronze and Iron Ages explored. Archaeological remains from the Late Bronze Age may suggest that Shiloh was the site of an isolated, hilltop cult place with no associated permanent settlement. Votive offerings of ceramic vessels and exotic small finds including a female figurine, a seal impression on a handle and a gold ornament depicting a fly may have been gifts to the cult place that were later buried and dumped onto the slope in the Iron Age I (Finkelstein 1993, 1367).

Although an actual sanctuary that could be related to the Iron Age I — when the biblical texts describe a cult place that housed the Ark of the Covenant — was not identified, the excavators did uncover contemporary pillared buildings that were not typical domestic structures. They interpret these structures as connected to the cult center at the site, and the associated fragments of a cult stand, vessels decorated with animal heads and many animal bones as evidence for cultic activities (Finkelstein 1993, 383–85). The excavators concluded from the presence of this specialized material — and the only known public architecture in the central highlands dating to the Iron Age I — that Shiloh served as a cult center that was at the peak of its prosperity in the first half of the eleventh century BCE and abandoned at the end of the eleventh century BCE (Finkelstein 1993, 386–89).

We learn from Judg. 21.19 and 1 Sam. 1.3 that the feast at Shiloh was an annual event. The latter passage, which describes the actions of Elkanah, states: "Now this man used to go up year by year from his town to worship and to sacrifice to the Lord of hosts at Shiloh . . ." We also learn in 1 Samuel 1 that Elkanah took his two wives, Hannah and Peninah, with him to the annual sacrifice, and that one year, the infertile Hannah vowed to Yahweh that she would dedicate her son to the sanctuary if Yahweh would allow her to conceive. Several years later, after Hannah has borne Samuel and weaned him (see above), she brings the boy along with other sacrifices to the shrine. We learn in 1 Sam. 2.19 that Hannah and Elkanah continued to go to Shiloh every year, in part to bring their son new clothes. It is clear from the passages in 1 Samuel 1, as well as those in Judges 21, that both men and women participated in this important cultic event in early Israel.

The act of visiting shrines to ask for help in getting pregnant continued into the late twentieth century among elderly women of Middle Eastern origin living in Jerusalem. One of the most common reasons why these women visited the tombs of ancestors, most often saints, was to request the saint's assistance for a female relative who is having trouble getting pregnant (Sered 1992, 24). The women report that young women who cannot bear children also make trips to these shrines, and promise to hold their unborn sons' bar mitzvahs at the saint's tomb if their vow is granted (25). Pregnant women also make trips to these shrines for the belief that it has a positive effect on the fetus (26).

It is unlikely that everyone in the land participated in the annual event at Shiloh, however, since some must have stayed behind in the villages to protect the land and other property. It is also possible that places of pilgrimage, including Shiloh, did not have the necessary space or facilities to support such a large influx of people (Haran 1977, 294). Regardless, the annual pilgrimage to Shiloh was the most important holiday of the year. Celebrated at the end of the harvest and just before the rainy season began, it was a time when farmers could get away from their fields for a few days or a week (Haran 1977, 298–300). The olive harvest would have been an ideal time for such a celebration, as ripening olives do not have to be picked immediately and the family can afford to leave for a few days if someone stays behind to protect the groves.

Although women's religious lives and the variety of women's religious experiences are not described in detail by the biblical authors, we can imagine that they focused more on practice in the home (see Chapter 3) than public worship. Women could not serve as priests in ancient Israel, and they were restricted in other ways from participating in the official cult, in part because purity laws may have prevented them from participating in religious activities during menstruation, after childbirth and at other impure times. From the story of Hannah we learn that nursing a child might take precedence over religious obligations. It is possible that most women would have been too inconvenienced or simply unable to participate in religious activities outside of the home because of their overwhelming contributions to the household and the constant demands of pregnancy, nursing and childcare.

The biblical writers do describe women in public religious roles, however. In Israel's early history, Miriam had a role in the cult of Yahweh (Num. 12.1-5) and women served in the Tabernacle in the period of the Exodus (Exod. 38.8). During the period of the monarchy, women were devotees of the Canaanite goddess Astarte (Jer. 7.16-20; 44.15-19) and the Mesopotamian god Tammuz (Ezek. 8.14); professional female mourners are mentioned in Jer. 9:17 (see Chapter 7). Women could also be prophetesses: in the period of the Judges, Deborah was a prophetess as well as a Judge, and the female prophets Huldah and Noadiah are known from the period of the monarchy and the post-exilic period respectively. The biblical writers did not consider these female prophets unusual, and the texts even reveal that Deborah (Judg. 4.4) and Huldah (2 Kgs 22.14) were married, as would have been expected of all women in ancient Israel. Women could also serve as mediums, as in the case of the woman at Endor (1 Sam. 28.7-25); in the story, Saul visits the medium and asks her to conjure up the spirit of the dead Samuel in her home, despite prohibitions against this practice (Exod. 22.18; Deut. 18.10-11) (see Chapter 7). Female diviners are also condemned in Ezek. 13.17-18, which shows that they were operating in ancient Israel.[10]

Unlike men, women who served as prophetesses, judges, mourners, mediums, diviners and other cultic personnel in ancient Israel probably practiced their calling on a part-time basis since their primary roles were those of wife and mother. It is possible that women did not take on such roles until later in life, after their childbearing years (Bird 1997, 41; see further Chapter 7); midwives, who were also ritual experts (see Chapter 5), were likely older women who had much experience with childbirth. The annual event at Shiloh, which specifically included women (1 Sam. 1.3-8), was not an isolated opportunity for them to participate in the cult, but it was one of only a few valid possibilities according to the biblical writers. As it was for Hannah, Orah's participation in the pilgrimage to Shiloh has a fertility aspect:

it was an opportunity to thank Yahweh for the gift of children by offering gifts to him at his most important shrine.

For Further Reading

Bird, P. 1997. *Missing Persons and Mistaken Identities: Women and Gender in Ancient Israel*. Minneapolis: Augsburg Fortress. An important collection of the author's studies on women in the Hebrew Bible from a feminist perspective. Includes Bird's influential study of the roles of women in Israelite religion.

Finkelstein, I., S. Bunimovitz and Z. Lederman, eds. 1993. *Shiloh: The Archaeology of a Biblical Site*. Tel Aviv: Tel Aviv University. A report of Tel Aviv University's archaeological excavations at the biblical site of Shiloh. Includes reports of the stratigraphy and architecture, pottery and other small finds, with additional studies on the ancient economy and environment.

Frankel, R., S. Avitsur and E. Ayalon. 1994. *History and Technology of Olive Oil in the Holy Land*. Trans. J.C. Jacobson. Tel Aviv: Eretz Israel Museum. A thorough and well-illustrated study of olive oil production in Israel in antiquity that includes information gleaned from ethnographic research in Palestine in the nineteenth and twentieth centuries.

Haran, M. 1977. *Temples and Temple-Service in Ancient Israel: An Inquiry into Biblical Cult Phenomena and the Historical Setting of the Priestly School*. Oxford: Clarendon Press. An analysis of Israelite temples and cult places and the textual evidence for the cults practiced within them. Includes a chapter on the three pilgrim feasts and family festivals celebrated in ancient Israel.

Notes

1 Graham-Brown 1980, chapter 1, photo 23; Granqvist 1947, 121–22; Grant 1907, frontispiece.

2 For more on pillar figurines, see Kletter 1996.

3 The meaning of Isa. 28.9-10 is uncertain, but it could reflect the idea that children at the age of weaning can be taught to read and write. It reads, "Whom will he teach knowledge, and to whom will he explain the message? Those who are weaned from milk, those taken from the breast? For it is precept upon precept, precept upon precept, line upon line, line upon line, here a little, there a little."

4 The Hebrew term *meshiah*, "messiah," means one who is anointed with oil.

5 Graham-Brown 1980, chapter 1, photo 32; Grant 1907, 38.

6 Graham-Brown 1980, chapter 1, photo 36.

7 For more on olives and the technology of oil production in ancient Israel, see Frankel, *et al.* 1994.

8 See King and Stager 2001, 163 for discussion.

9 See further van Driel-Murray 2000.

10 For more on women's religious lives, see Meyers 2005.

Chapter 7

Old Age and Death

Orah's Story

It is the feeling of helplessness that troubles Orah the most, and the fact that she is unable to contribute to the household like she has for nearly all of her life. Her hands hurt a great deal now, as does her lower back; both are the result of a lifetime of manual work. She can no longer grind grain on her grinding stones next to her daughter Hilah and her daughter-in-law, make and decorate pottery or do the countless other things that are required to keep her son's household running. But work is essentially all she knows, and so she stubbornly persists in helping as much as she can with the daily chores, even though she winces and sometimes even cries out in pain while kneeling next to the indoor hearth or climbing the ladder up to the second floor to sleep in the cold evenings.

Despite her physical deterioration, Orah is the matron of her son's household, and is due a great deal of respect from all of the people who live in it, including her son. At nearly 40 years of age, Orah has already survived her husband by several years, and she continues to live in the house where she and her husband spent all of their adult lives. The makeup of the household has changed much during the many years she has lived here, and she has special knowledge of the family's ancestors, both those she knew in life and those who were already gone by the time she married her husband. As the oldest woman in the house, she has a say in important family decisions and is actively involved in marriage arrangements for her daughter Hilah, who is now the age Orah had been when her parents arranged for her marriage. As one of the oldest women in the village, Orah is revered as the mother of two children and even a grandmother; it was rare indeed for a woman to know her own grandchildren, and Orah was fortunate to have been blessed with a grandson.

It is rainy and windy in the early winter, and Orah spends most of her time indoors trying to keep warm by the hearth in the central room on the ground floor. One overcast day while her daughter and daughter-in-law are occupied on the second floor and her son is sowing seeds in the field for next year's wheat crop with the other men of the village, Orah notices that more water is needed for the evening meal, and so she picks up an empty jar and carries it down the path to the spring outside of the village. Although she is somehow able to fill the jar partway by herself, she slips and falls in the mud when she tries to balance the vessel on her head to carry it back to the house. She is cold, scared and humiliated when her daughter-in-law finds her some time later. Her daughter-in-law runs quickly back to the village to call for help, and several women abandon their work to help carry Orah back to the house. There, Orah's daughter-in-law and Hilah wrap her in a blanket and examine Orah's leg, which is clearly broken. Hilah finds the small jar of honey and applies some to the wound and does her best to splint and wrap her leg. That night, Orah's bed is made by the hearth and her son and Hilah sit nervously by her side. They both know that their mother may not recover from this accident.

Orah sleeps poorly that night and is in a great deal of pain. Unable to do anything else to ease her suffering, her son walks to a neighboring village early the next morning to request the services of a sorceress. The woman, who is quite advanced in age as well, is known to have special powers, and the villagers sometimes call upon her to heal the sick. By the time she and Orah's son reach Orah, her leg is quite inflamed and swollen and the sorceress can do little but apply more honey while chanting healing prayers over her. She gives Orah a sip of liquid from a juglet that takes some of the pain away, and she watches and waits while Orah sleeps fitfully through the afternoon. Seeing no change and understanding that Orah's condition is grave, the sorceress returns to her village that evening, leaving Orah in the care of Hilah. Orah is feverish that night and talks incoherently of her long-dead sister and mother, while Hilah attempts to keep her comfortable with cool, wet cloths and soothing words. Attended by her daughter, who dozes on the floor next to her mother, Orah dies peacefully the third night after the accident, simply too weak to survive the infection that has developed in her broken leg.

Hilah is weeping when the family awakens early the next morning, and they all understand immediately that Orah is gone. Her son kneels over her body and says a blessing over it before cutting the hem of his cloak and the edge of his beard with a flint blade. Hilah and Orah's daughter-in-law smear ashes from the hearth on their faces and clothes and begin their loud laments; before long, the neighbors hear the noise coming from the house and soon nearly everyone in the village gathers in the courtyard or main room of the house to lament the loss of the old woman. Orah's son and the other men leave soon after, as women are responsible for preparing the body for burial according to the traditions of the village. The task falls to Hilah and her sister-in-law, who remove Orah's clothing and jewelry, wash and rub her body with olive oil and dress her in the brightly colored garment she wore on feast days. They move the body to the rear room of the house before lighting incense on the altar to invoke the presence of the goddess, and Hilah and her sister-in-law tie the old amulet around Orah's neck that protected her during the birth of her children; Orah's spirit is vulnerable during this transitional time, and the women hope the presence of the deity and the powerful amulet will protect her. After wrapping her body in a thin woolen shroud and securing it with a bronze pin, they join the neighbor women in preparing a meal that will be consumed after the burial that evening.

As dusk approaches, Orah's son carries her wrapped body to an area on the edge of the fields marked by a cypress tree; this is the village cemetery, and Orah's son has already dug a shallow pit near the other graves that are marked with upright field stones. His father is buried here along with several other ancestors and the dozens who have died since the founding of the village. The rest of the villagers follow him, some carrying torches to light the way, others carrying gifts of food and drink that will be placed in the tomb along with the body. After the body is laid in the grave, Hilah places bowls of food and drink around it along with a handstone that Orah had used in her final years to grind grain for the family. The village women fall on their knees and weep loudly next to the grave as Hilah and her sister-in-law fill it with earth; the men remain at a distance from the grave until it is closed and a simple upright stone is placed at one end. For seven days thereafter, the village women will return to the grave with more food and drink offerings; they believe that the dead need sustenance, and hope that their simple contributions, which include leftover bits of meat and vegetables from the funerary feast, will be acceptable to Orah's spirit.

After the first week Hilah and her sister-in-law are the only regular visitors to the grave. Hilah can often be seen sitting next to the marking stone, talking to her deceased mother about the goings-on of the household and the plans for her upcoming wedding. Other women from the village visit the grave occasionally, usually when they are in need of special favors; Orah continues to be revered for her fertility even in death, and young women who have trouble conceiving visit the grave with food offerings and ask for her help. As the years pass and there are fewer and fewer visitors to the tomb, the bowls that have accumulated on the surface are broken and mixed with vessels from other graves, and the fallen marking stone is taken and reused to mark the grave of another villager some years later. All memory of Orah's tomb is lost after the passing of two generations, when her great-grandchildren move to towns and cities throughout the land; eventually, all of the remains of Orah and her burial place will be lost through millennia of agricultural activity. But even after all physical traces of her existence have disappeared her name is remembered by her female descendants, who tell their daughters about a woman named Orah who lived and died in a small village in Israel in the time before kings, a woman who, in spirit, gave birth to them all.

Introduction

We are not told many details about the lives of older people in the Hebrew Bible, and most biblical offerings of respect to the elderly are directed specifically toward men. We can probably assume that the elderly were contributing members of the early Israelite household until their health deteriorated, and it appears from the texts that they were respected in their communities for their wisdom. Leviticus 19.32, for example, states: "You shall rise before the aged, and defer to the old; and you shall fear your God: I am the Lord," while Deut. 32.7 calls on the people of Israel to "[r]emember the days of old, consider the years long past; ask your father, and he will inform you; your elders, and they will tell you." An idyllic passage about old age (Zech. 8.4) refers to old men and women sitting in the squares of Jerusalem with their walking sticks (King and Stager 2001, 58). Given what we know of the healing practices of the time, however, old age was probably not a pleasant experience for most.

The biblical writers describe some of the illnesses associated with old age. Barzillai, for example, who claimed to be 80 years old, suffered from a dulled sense of taste and was hard of hearing (2 Sam. 19.35). Blindness is also associated with advanced age (Gen. 27.1-2), as is the inability to keep warm (1 Kgs 1.2) and, of course, diminished fertility (Gen. 18.13). According to a number of biblical passages, illness was seen as the result of Yahweh's whims, and one could only be healed by offering prayers to Yahweh in one of his temples (see below). Other avenues of treatment, like the services of a sorceress, were available however, and home remedies were certainly known. In our story, Orah's infection in her leg, coupled with her poor physical condition, could not be effectively treated with remedies available at the time; when prayer did not work, there was little else that could have been done to heal her leg and prolong her life.

When an older woman is described by the biblical writers, she is usually described as a widow (*'almana*). It is believed that the average lifespan of an ancient Israelite woman was about 30 years, and many women died young because of the dangers of childbirth. There may have been many widows in ancient Israel because of the age difference between a man and a woman when they married; men are believed to have been eight or ten years older than their wives,[1] making widows more common than widowers even after taking into account women's low life expectancy. Even though widows were considered vulnerable and even inferior members of society according to the biblical writers (see below), they, like everyone else in ancient Israel, were due proper mourning, burial and mortuary rituals. In our story, Orah's family and the women of the village dutifully perform these acts upon her death.

Widowhood

According to a number of biblical passages, widows were in need of Yahweh's protection, in part because they did not necessarily have family members to protect them. In over half of the references to widows in the Hebrew Bible, the *'almana* is grouped together with the fatherless and the client (also translated as "stranger"), which were two other threatened segments of society (Hiebert 1989, 126–27). Yahweh's protection of these groups is seen, for example, in Ps. 146.9: "The Lord watches over the strangers; he upholds the orphans and the widow, but the way of the wicked he brings to ruin." Yahweh also provides protection by demanding that gleanings from the fields be set aside for the fatherless, clients and widows (Lev. 19.9-10; Deut. 24.21). Like the client — a man who is living outside of the geographical area of his kin — a widow did not have blood ties with the members of her deceased husband's household; this put her in a tenuous position, as no male had direct authority over her. This is evident in Num. 30.6-9, which states that a woman's vow needs to be approved by either her father or her husband, but a widow or divorced woman could make the vow on her own (Hiebert 1989, 130). Although it seems from this passage like a widow's independence could be an advantage, widowhood was far from an ideal situation according to the biblical writers.

Widows were apparently set apart by wearing special clothing, such as in Gen. 38.14, where Tamar ". . . put off her widow's garments, put on a veil, wrapped herself up, and sat down at the entrance to Enaim . . ." in an effort to appear like a prostitute when she seduced her father-in-law Judah. Upon leaving Judah, she took off her veil and put on her widow's clothes once more (Gen. 38.19). These may be similar to garments worn by women who were in mourning for other reasons; 2 Sam. 21.10 records that Rizpah, Saul's concubine, prepared sackcloth for herself to wear in mourning after her sons were handed over to the Gibeonites. Although we cannot guess the color of a widow's garments, it seems that they were made of rougher material than was typically used to make clothing, and were perhaps identifiable to others in some other way.

Widows without children were protected by levirate marriage, which required that a childless widow marry one of her deceased husband's brothers in order to continue the family line of her dead husband and pass on his land inheritance, or *nahala*. This was seen as a widow's right, and perhaps the only chance a woman would have for security after the death of her husband (Marsman 2003, 316). Three passages in the Hebrew Bible describe levirate marriage: the story of Tamar and Judah (Genesis 38), the laws in Deut. 25.5-10 and possibly the story of Ruth and Boaz. The story of Tamar and Judah in Genesis 38 especially shows the lengths a woman may have gone to ensure that her dead husband's line was continued and his inheritance preserved.

In the story, Tamar's husband, Er, has died before they could conceive a child and she is under the authority of her father-in-law, Judah, who is required to arrange a marriage between her and one of his other sons so that she might conceive with one of them. When his second oldest son Onan is unwilling (and killed by Yahweh as a result of his behavior) and the third son deemed too young for marriage, Judah sends Tamar back to her father's house. Some time later, when Tamar hears that Judah's wife has died, she decides to trick Judah into having sex with her by disguising herself as a prostitute so that she can provide progeny for her dead husband. Her plan succeeds (Gen. 38.6-19). The other biblical passage that clearly describes levirate marriage confirms that it was to be taken seriously. According to Deut. 25.7-10, a widow could bring her case to court if a brother-in-law would not perform his duty; if the unwilling brother-in-law denounced his right, the widow could marry whomever she wished (Marsman 2003, 317).

The story of Tamar and Judah shows the tremendous importance of inheritance in ancient Israelite society; indeed, one of the main reasons why widows were so vulnerable is that inheritance laws did not provide for them. In general, a man's property went to his nearest male relative or relatives, usually his sons, upon his death; only in exceptional cases did daughters receive an inheritance from their fathers, such as in the story of Zelophehad and his five daughters (Num. 27.1-11). In this story, which was apparently a legal precedent because it is mentioned in multiple biblical passages (Josh. 17.3-6; 1 Chron. 7.15), the daughters of the deceased Zelophehad were allowed to inherit their father's *nahala* if they married within their own tribe, thus ensuring that the land inheritance would remain within the clan (Borowski 2003, 82). A man could, however, make arrangements to provide for his wife after his death, perhaps by giving his wife all or part of the dowry she brought to the marriage. This was apparently the case with Nabal's widow, Abigail, who had five maids (1 Sam. 25.42), and Micah's widowed mother, who owned 1,100 pieces of silver (Judg. 17.1-4) (Marsman 2003, 308). Since gifts of land were only exchanged by rich families, it is believed that a woman's dowry typically included slaves and other movable goods, which would not provide a woman with enough to support herself for a long period of time (Hiebert 1989, 136). As in marriage arrangements, a woman from a wealthy family was surely in a better situation than a woman from a poor family when her husband died.

Although the biblical writers focus on the challenges faced by the widow, we should understand that widows were due respect in their households and communities. Family matriarchs almost certainly had a say in important family decisions, as seen, for example, in the story of Rebekah, whose widowed mother and brother arrange for her marriage (see Chapter 4). Women were ritual experts in their relationships with the dead especially (see below), and they may have played important roles in the household cult as well. Certainly older women were keepers of family traditions, and they transferred family stories and songs to their progeny along with knowledge of crafts and technologies and religious practices. Elderly women were an important connection to a family's past; given the reverence for ancestors in ancient Israelite tradition, this put them in a uniquely important position within their households.

Widows with grown children were able to pursue careers that took them outside their homes and communities. Midwives, for example, were usually older women who were able to professionalize once freed of the burden of raising young children (see Chapter 5), and older women with lightened household responsibilities may have become other kinds of healthcare practitioners — like sorceresses — as well. In exceptional cases, older women, including widows, went on to participate in the public cult as prophetesses, for example (see Chapter 6). Since it is believed that a primary reason why women were "held back" from taking on public roles was their overwhelming and largely unavoidable responsibilities to their father's and later husband's households, it is likely that once freed of some of these responsibilities, talented women could have gone on to hold public religious roles even during the period of the monarchy.

This idea persisted into the twentieth century among elderly Sephardic women living in Jerusalem. They viewed their widowhood positively, as it freed them from the demands of their husbands and allowed them to develop their public religious lives in ways that were not previously possible. Women without husbands and young children to care for are able to participate in public worship in their synagogue and make more frequent trips to holy shrines; their participation in public rituals is intended to protect their family members, and they believe that such rituals are more efficacious when performed in public locations (Sered 1992, 110). Elderly women, especially those with sons, also had increased status in their communities even if they did not become more powerful in political or religious matters. It must be noted, however, that women living in modern Israel had a much greater life expectancy than women living in the "old country," and having an active religious life in old age is a relatively recent phenomenon for most (Sered 1992, 109).

Two of the characters in our story are widows: Orah's grandmother (Chapter 1) and Orah at the end of her life. Both are mothers to older children when their husbands die, and both continue to live in their husband's households under the protection of their sons. Their situations are thus more secure than that of a young, childless woman, and their advanced age and special knowledge make them entitled to respect from their families and communities. In her final days, Orah is involved in making marriage arrangements for her daughter Hilah, demonstrating her important role in family decision making even at the end of her life. As one of the oldest women in her village when she dies, she is especially revered as someone who has been blessed with two surviving children and a grandson, and she continues to be revered even after her death by the women in her community.

Health and Medicine

Health was generally poor because hygiene was inadequate by our standards in ancient Israel as in the rest of the ancient world. Nevertheless health was probably better in the small, sparsely populated highland villages than in the crowded cities of the succeeding Iron Age II. Regardless, Orah lived to an age likely unseen by most women in antiquity who were not royalty or otherwise privileged, and nearly 40 years of labor in the house and in the fields has weakened her body and her resistance. When she develops an infection in her leg, it is treated with the application of honey, which has antibiotic properties, and the sorceress and the members of the household pray for Orah's recovery. The sorceress gives Orah a drink from a juglet — perhaps strong wine or some other alcoholic drink — to dull her pain, but the drink is not curative and it does little to improve her situation. Orah's exposure to the elements after her fall and the drafty conditions in her house were also not conducive to the healing process, although it is unlikely that she would have survived the accident even in better weather.

According to the biblical passages, personal cleanliness involved regularly washing one's hands, face and feet, but the entire body was rarely immersed in water or cleansed except for times when purity demanded it (see Chapter 3). Clothing was rarely washed and changed; indeed, many probably lacked a change of clothing (Chapter 4) and outer garments were used as blankets as well. Sanitation in houses and settlements was generally poor, with garbage probably dumped in alleys and other outdoor spaces (2 Sam. 22.43). Disease would have been spread by the animals and insects that found ideal breeding grounds in the refuse near household compounds. The close proximity of stabled animals and their dung in indoor and outdoor cooking spaces spread bacteria, as did shared food bowls; dishes were cleaned by rubbing with sand or perhaps with a quick rinse in water if it could be spared. The biblical writers do mention several cleaning compounds, including *neter*, which is probably a mixture of natron — a sort of salt mixture — and *borit*, lye (Jer. 2.22, Job 9.30) (Neufeld 1971, 54–55), but we do not have the physical evidence for their use, and can assume that the population of early Israel was dirty most of the time by our standards.

Ancient skeletal remains vividly illustrate the effects that harsh working conditions had on female and male bodies in antiquity. Musculoskeletal stress markers resulting from use of certain upper arm and back muscles may correlate to repetitive activities like grinding grain that may have occupied many women up to several hours per day (see Chapter 2). A study of prehistoric and Early Bronze Age I skeletons from the southern Levant suggests that food processing activities that relied on well-developed upper-body musculature increased in women in the Early Bronze Age from the Neolithic period, as people became more reliant on domesticated plants and animals (Peterson 2002, 124–25). Although this damage could have resulted from other work, it seems likely given what we know of women's food processing tasks in Bronze and Iron Age villages that grinding grain could have had a deleterious effect on women's health. In the case of a woman of advanced age like Orah, these injuries may have weakened her resistance, making her unable to fight the more immediate health threats she faced when she broke her leg.

Illness was a divine instrument in ancient Israel (Exod. 7-10), and the sick sought reconciliation with Yahweh, through prayer or otherwise, as part of the healing process (Avalos 1995, 244). Infertility, as seen in the story of Hannah in 1 Samuel 1, was considered a sickness that required a petition to Yahweh (Avalos 1995, 327–28) or to deceased ancestors (see further below). According to the biblical writers, medical care was largely the responsibility of religious practitioners, but in reality, "the home was the only or main locus of healthcare for most of the duration of an illness" (Avalos 1995, 251). Sick royalty, for example, were cared for at home, as in the cases of David and Bathsheba's son (2 Sam. 12.15-18), Hezekiah (2 Kgs 20) and Amnon, who feigned illness as a ploy to bring Tamar to his room (2 Sam. 13.5); those of high status, such as the son of the Shunammite woman who is resuscitated by the prophet Elisha (2 Kgs 4.8-37), were also treated at home.

Home remedies derived from plants were certainly known in ancient Israel. Among them was terebinth resin, which was used as a medicine and exported to Egypt (Gen. 37.25) and Phoenicia (Ezek. 27.17); frankincense and myrrh also had medicinal uses (King and Stager 2001, 80–81). Burning incense in the home would have helped rid the area of flies and mosquitoes and, in doing so, prevent the spread of disease. Mandrakes were used to cure infertility in Gen. 30.14-16. The analysis of residues on a Late Bronze Age juglet made in Cyprus and imported to the site of Tell el-Ajjul, now in the Gaza Strip, identified the remains of opium (Merrillees and Evans 1989, 148*–54*). The opium poppy was not native to ancient Palestine, and we still have no context for the use of opium in ancient Canaan and Israel; we do not know if it was used as a painkiller in medical treatments, in religious contexts or for recreation. As they are in many other traditional societies, women were likely the keepers of knowledge of medicinal plants and other pharmaceuticals in ancient Israelite households.

Health practitioners who had special knowledge of medical treatments, like midwives (Chapter 5), functioned in ancient Israel, as did healthcare consultants considered illegitimate by the biblical writers. Among those illegitimate practitioners were sorcerers, the only group from among the list of condemned cultic professions in Deut. 18.10-12 for whom female practitioners are mentioned (Exod. 22.18; Isa. 57.3) (Meyers 2005, 65). These women might have "used their magic to function as 'health care consultants,' or folk healers, who could use various potions and herbal substances along with incantations to treat illness and exorcize evil spirits" (Meyers 2000d, 197). They may have competed with legitimate Yahwistic consultants for clients, which led to denouncements and laws against them (Avalos 1995, 297).

Other illegitimate healthcare consultants included the dead. People commonly consulted the dead about various matters in ancient Israel, such as when Saul visits a female medium at Endor to ask questions of the deceased Samuel (see below). The dead had the power to give and revive life, and were thus appeased by the living through the offering of food and drink (Bloch-Smith 1992a, 122–23). It is possible that dead ancestors were believed to have the ability to give fertility blessings, which may be behind the story of Hannah's prayer for a child during the sacrifice at Shiloh (Bloch-Smith 1992a, 122).[2] These consultations are condemned in numerous biblical passages (Lewis 1989), showing that they were probably widely practiced in ancient Israel. In our story, after the initial week of mourning, Orah's tomb is visited only infrequently by the women of her village who are not family members; these visits have the primary purpose of plying Orah's spirit with food and drink with the hope that she will grant women fertility. Since Orah has lived long enough to see a grandson — something quite unusual in ancient Israel given women's live expectancy — it was believed that she had special powers of fertility that she could bestow upon others. Such tomb visitations are within the realm of funerary ritual, those actions performed by the living in response to the death of a member of the family or community.

Funerary Rituals

Archaeological remains, along with the Hebrew Bible, which is replete with images of death and burial, are the best sources we have for reconstructing Israelite funerary rituals and burial practices. Unfortunately, we know much less about burial practices during the Iron Age I than we do about practices in the Late Bronze Age and Iron Age II because there are many fewer Iron Age I burials.[3] Given what we know of early and later burial practices and beliefs, however, we can assume that the Iron I dead were not exposed, cremated or treated in other ways alien to ancient Israel; instead, it appears that part of the Iron I population was buried in Bronze Age burial caves and other cemeteries used for millennia. According to the texts, the ideal burial situation was the ancestral tomb; the matriarchs and patriarchs of Genesis, for example, were buried in cave tombs, including the Cave at Machpelah (Bloch-Smith 1992a, 87). Typically, when a body was interred in a cave tomb, skeletal remains and artifacts were pushed to the cave periphery to clear the central space for the recently deceased and his or her grave goods. Because many cave tombs were used for long periods of time, human remains and grave goods are found mixed and it is not always possible to assign a date to individual burials.

Others were buried in simple pit graves that have since been destroyed or are located in open agricultural areas rarely explored by archaeologists (Faust 2004, 175–76), and individual interments seem to have been practiced only when someone was on the road or otherwise away from home. In our story, Orah is buried in a simple pit grave in a burial ground outside of the village on the edge of the fields, as there are no Bronze Age burial caves located in the vicinity. Since the dead were called upon by family members and villagers for various reasons, it was important that her grave be located in close proximity to her village. The small cemetery is marked by an old cypress tree; interment near a tree is attested several times in the Hebrew Bible (Gen. 35.8; 1 Sam. 31.12-13) and may be related to the concept of the tree of life (Bloch-Smith 1992a, 113–15). In the Hebrew Bible, tombs are considered a physical witness to land ownership (Josh. 24.30; Judg. 2.9), further demonstrating the importance of the *nahala* in ancient Israelite society.

We can learn about the treatment of the body immediately after death from the biblical sources. The body needed to be dealt with quickly, following the funerary prescription of burying the deceased on the day of death when possible, which was a necessity in a hot climate (King and Stager 2001, 364). The body was possibly handled by the women in the household for reasons of purity; men and women who handled corpses were considered impure for at least a week (Num. 19.11-13), and it is possible that women were more likely to perform this act because women were more commonly in states of impurity. Women's handling of the corpse might be considered a continuation of women's care of family members generally. The body was washed and rubbed with oil before it was dressed and adorned; we can imagine that the dead were dressed in the garments worn at the time of death, or they could have worn special garments that marked their status. The dead were adorned with jewelry they had worn in life, like metal anklets (see Chapter 3) and amulets (see Chapter 5); jewelry comprises the second largest category of artifacts found in Iron Age tombs (Bloch-Smith 1992b: 218–19). Evidence that bodies were wrapped in a cloak or a piece of fabric might be seen in the story of the medium of Endor, as Samuel's spirit is wearing a cloak when it is conjured for Saul, who identifies him. Toggle pins and fibulae of bronze would have been used to secure the cloaks or wrappings (Bloch-Smith 1992b, 218).

Since Orah was quite old and her family had been preparing for her death, the grave goods had already been prepared for her so the burial event was not done in haste. At sundown she was laid in the grave after being carried out in a procession led by her son. Food and drink offerings were buried with her in bowls, and a handstone that she had used in life accompanies her as well; one of the bowls had been made and decorated by Orah herself with the geometric motifs she learned from her father's concubine long ago. These simple offerings reflect the need to provision the dead with sustenance in the afterlife and ensure that the deceased is accompanied with something that reflects his or her life (Ebeling 2002). The interment was followed by a funerary meal eaten in Orah's house because of the bad weather; this meal, which was prepared by female relatives and neighbors, could also have been

140

consumed graveside. Leftovers from this meal were sometimes placed in tombs before they were closed (see below).

The tradition of providing food at meals eaten in celebration of the dead continues until today, and for elderly women living in modern Jerusalem it is the job of the female relatives to serve food and drink to visitors to the house of mourning for a week following a death. The central mourning ritual in the women's space in segregated houses concerns food, and women respond to the death "by strengthening interpersonal ties through preparing and serving food to friends and kin" (Sered 1992, 100). It is traditional to eat certain foods during the period of mourning, including round foods like lentils and eggs, which symbolize death and rebirth, and mourners cannot eat anything from their own house during this time (Sered 1992, 100–1).

According to Gen. 50.10, mourning took place for seven days, and various mourning rituals described in the Hebrew Bible might have been practiced by family members and villagers during this period. Mourning rituals included tearing the clothes (2 Sam. 1.11), fasting (2 Sam. 1.12), wearing rough clothing (2 Sam. 3.31), tearing out the hair and beard (Jer. 7.29), rolling in ashes (Jer. 6.26), sitting on the ground (Lam. 2.10) and gashing the skin (Deut. 14.1). Jeremiah 9.17-20 refers to skilled women who are professional mourners, showing that women's mourning was a specialized craft or profession. Jeremiah calls on these skilled women to teach their mourning songs to their daughters and neighbors, which might literally refer to other members of their guilds. Chanting laments and perhaps composing them was thus a female activity in ancient Israel, and women specialized in performing these services when they were needed (Meyers 2000c, 327–28).

Other sources from the ancient Near East and Egypt demonstrate that women were employed as professional mourners who were hired to publicly recite laments for the dead as they accompanied funerary processions and other organized funeral activities. Images of mourning women with upraised arms are known from tomb paintings in Egypt, including a well-known image from the New Kingdom tomb of Ramose in Thebes that depicts women and girls with upraised arms, lamenting the deceased. Some Egyptian women had "mourner" as a title, which indicates that this was their occupation (Robins 1993, 164). In ancient Israel, several figurines depicting women with upraised arms have been found at seventh-century BCE Azor on the southern coast of Israel (see Figure 7.1). These may be images of women in mourning, although upraised arms could also represent worship, defeat and other things in ancient Israel. In our story, the women in Orah's household and village loudly mourn Orah's death in her house and during her funeral, and both women and men in the family express their sorrow physically in other ways.

7.1 Woman mourning (after Vamosh 2007, 68).

These public expressions of grief were expected in ancient Israel, and they served to mark this transformative occasion for all who witnessed it.

Mortuary Cult

In our story, the relationship between Orah and her family and community does not end with her death; after a period of mourning, her tomb is visited regularly by family members and some of the women in the village who are experiencing infertility. Deceased ancestors remained important to the family, and the Hebrew Bible preserves motives as well as methods for caring for them (Bloch-Smith 1992b, 221). The cult of the dead, as defined by Theodore Lewis, includes "those acts directed toward the deceased function-ing either to placate the dead or to secure favors from them for the present life" (Lewis 1989, 2). The dead were believed to have a number of special powers, and the biblical writers describe instances in which the dead were sought for information and favors.

The dead were believed by the ancient Israelites to live in a dark and gloomy underworld called *Sheol*. Often called a pit (Isa. 14.15), *Sheol* was located beneath the earth and specifically beneath Israel. It was similar to other Near Eastern conceptions of the netherworld in that it was unpleasant, democratic (everyone from kings to paupers went to *Sheol*) and, perhaps, ruled by a god and goddess of the dead[4] (Hallote 2001, 107–14). Various biblical passages inform on some of the beliefs surrounding *Sheol* as well as its physical description. The deceased who inhabited *Sheol* forgot about Yahweh and could not praise him (Ps. 6.5); in addition, and perhaps even worse, Yahweh did not remember the dead who lived there (Ps. 88.4-5). *Sheol* was a physical place that had a road leading to it, possessed a gate and was like a prison (Hallote 2001, 108–9). Needless to say, the living feared this place.

The best biblical example of the living consulting the dead is found in 1 Samuel 28, when Saul consults with a female medium at Endor to conjure up the spirit of the dead Samuel. Although consulting mediums was forbidden according to Exod. 22.18 and Deut. 18.10-14, and Saul even outlawed them himself (1 Sam. 28.9), he inquired of the dead Samuel about the outcome of his impending battle with the Philistines. After complaining that Saul has disturbed his sleep, Samuel predicts the defeat of the Israelites and the deaths of Saul and his sons (1 Sam. 28.19). Inquiring of the dead is described in other biblical passages; the dead not only tell the future and heal the sick, but they also invoke blessings of fertility, revive the dead and exact vengeance (Bloch-Smith 1992a, 121–22). That the dead were considered divine beings is indicated in the story of Saul and Samuel, where Samuel's apparition is called *'elohim*, literally "gods" (see also Isa. 8.19) (Bloch-Smith 1992b, 220).

In order to appease the dead so that they might help the living, the family continued to provide the deceased with food and drink. Sacrifices were offered to the ancestors at the tomb and in various other places, including at burial markers (Gen. 28.17-18), on hilltops (Gen. 31.53-54) and at shrines (1 Sam. 1.21; 20.6) (Bloch-Smith 1992b, 22–22). Offering food to the dead is described in a number of biblical passages, although offering tithed food was not acceptable to Yahweh (Deut. 26.14). Although the most common objects interred with the deceased during the Bronze and Iron Ages were ceramic vessels, identifying the archaeological remains of actual food and drink offerings is difficult because they usually do not preserve. Even when animal bones and residues from food and drink are identified in tomb vessels, it is impossible to know if they were buried in order to serve as sustenance in the afterlife or if they were the remains of a funerary meal. Regardless, the presence of it in tombs indicates that there was a belief that the dead required food and drink. Identifying the remains of such offerings left after the tomb was closed is impossible in the Iron Age I.[5]

The ethnographic evidence demonstrates that similar practices continued into the twentieth century in Israel. Middle Eastern women living in Jerusalem in the 1980s were reported to regularly visit the tombs of ancestors, especially those of saints, to seek "help in caring for both their living and their as yet unborn descendants" (Sered 1992, 19). These women living in modern Israel visit the graves on special days, including during the Festival of the New Moon and on the anniversaries of deaths, to cry over and kiss the graves and ask for mercy. Women light candles at the tomb if it is permitted by the Ministry of Religion, which controls these tombs, and leave small objects behind. Small bottles of oil left by previous pilgrims, for example, are taken home by the women and used as charms; they, in turn, might leave another bottle of oil, unlit candles, money or something representative of a family member needing the saint's intervention, or they might tie pieces of cloth onto the grating surrounding the tomb (Sered 1992, 118–19). If a petition that a woman has made on a previous trip to the tomb has been granted by the saint, the woman shares pieces of a cake that she has brought along with everyone in attendance, as she had promised if her vow was fulfilled. The ethnographer speculates that women's care and making requests of dead ancestors is an extension of women caring for their aging parents while they are still alive (Sered 1992, 22), and an important way that the women help their own loved ones (120).

Although the Israelite mortuary cult remained popular through the period of the monarchy, by the time of Isaiah such practices were considered to be among the worst of sins; the prophet warns: "I held out my hands all day long to a rebellious people, who walk in a way that is not good, following their own devices; a people who provoke me to my face continually . . . who sit inside tombs, and spend the night in secret places . . ." (Isa. 65.2-4). There are several reasons why the later biblical writers did not accept these mortuary practices. The mortuary cult practiced in Israel was essentially the same as the Canaanite cult of the dead, and the later monotheistic editors of the Hebrew Bible sought to divorce themselves from the practices of the polytheistic Canaanites (Hallote 2001, 64–65). In addition, the ancestral cult of the dead, with its focus on the importance of the original clans and tribes of Israel, threatened the unity formed by the kings during the monarchical period (Hallote 2001, 62). Offering sacrifices and asking favors of the dead were too similar to rituals performed to Yahweh — who legitimately healed the sick and made the infertile fertile — and made the dead too god-like according to the later biblical editors (Hallote 2001, 67–68). Despite the prohibitions against such activities in the eighth–seventh centuries BCE, however, the biblical and archaeological evidence suggests that the dead continued to be fed and consulted.

In our story Orah's family members and the women of the village visit her tomb regularly and bring offerings of food and drink. After her daughter Hilah marries and moves to another village and her son grows older and preoccupied with his responsibilities to the household, family visits to Orah's tomb become less frequent until finally the stone that marked the spot is lost along with the exact locations of other tombs in the small cemetery. After her progeny have moved to towns and cities and the small village is abandoned, Orah's final resting place will be lost, and after millennia of plowing activity all trace of her physical remains and the grave goods that accompanied her in death will be destroyed. Although this seems like an ignoble end, it is the memory of this woman in the minds of her family members that persists; the physical location of her remains is ultimately not so important.

For Further Reading

Avalos, H. 1995. *Illness and Health Care in the Ancient Near East: The Role of the Temple in Greece, Mesopotamia, and Israel*. Harvard Semitic Monographs 54, ed. P. Machinist. Atlanta: Scholars Press. A detailed discussion of beliefs about illness and healthcare practices in Mesopotamia and ancient Israel that focuses on the central role of the temple in diagnosis and subsequent care.

Bloch-Smith, E. 1992. *Judahite Burial Practices and Beliefs about the Dead*. Sheffield: Sheffield Academic Press. The definitive study of Iron Age burials that investigates how the archaeological remains contribute to our understanding of the mortuary practices and beliefs, including the cult of the dead, described in the Hebrew Bible.

Hallote, R.S. 2001. *Death, Burial, and Afterlife in the Biblical World: How the Israelites and Their Neighbors Treated the Dead*. Chicago: Ivan R. Dee. An accessible study of burial practices in ancient Israel and neighboring lands with a chapter on the politics of death in modern Israel.

Hiebert, P.S. 1989. "Whence Shall Help Come to Me?" The Biblical Widow. In *Gender and Difference in Ancient Israel*, ed. P.L. Day, 125–41. Minneapolis: Augsburg Fortress. Considers the status of the widow in ancient Israelite society through an examination of the Hebrew Bible and other ancient Near Eastern texts.

Lewis, T.J. 1989. *Cults of the Dead in Ancient Israel and Ugarit*. Ed. F.M. Cross. Harvard Semitic Monographs No. 39. Atlanta: Scholars Press. A study of the evidence for the Israelite cult of the dead in light of the texts from Ugarit.

Notes

1 Or ten to 15 years older, according to King and Stager 2001, 12.

2 Bloch-Smith believes that Hannah's family's participation in the festival at Shiloh is part of a "family sacrifice" (1 Sam. 20.29) that is a sacrifice for the ancestors (Bloch-Smith 1992a, 122).

3 Some have argued that the reason there are few burials is because Iron Age I society was poorer or more egalitarian than Iron Age II society (see Kletter 2002; Faust 2006). Regardless of the reasons for the scarcity of Iron Age I burials, we can reconstruct some of the burial customs of the period using archaeological data from earlier and later periods as well as the biblical sources.

4 The god and goddess who ruled the underworld may be evident, for example, in Isa. 28.15: ". . . We have made a covenant with death, and with She'ol we have an agreement" and Isa. 28.17-19: "And I will make justice the line, and righteousness the plummet . . . Then your covenant with Death will be annulled, and your agreement with She'ol will not stand . . ." (Hallote 2001, 114).

5 Excavations at Ugarit, on the Syrian coast, in the early twentieth century revealed holes and ceramic pipes in the ceilings and walls of tombs, which excavator Claude Schaeffer interpreted as evidence that the dead were regularly provided with food and drink. Reanalysis of the archaeological data has demonstrated that these installations are not related to the mortuary cult, and are instead the remains of drainage installations and other structures that served the houses above the tombs (Pitard 1994).

Conclusion

In this book, I have shown how various sources of evidence can be used to reconstruct one woman's life in an ancient Israelite village of the Iron Age I. Using archaeology, the Hebrew Bible and other ancient Near Eastern texts, iconography and ethnography from the modern Middle East, I described seven stages in Orah's life from the period following her birth in her father's village to her death in the household of her son. The events in Orah's story followed the agricultural cycle by which the ancient Israelites lived, and each chapter highlighted four events, activities or traditions relevant to the stage of Orah's life described in each narrative section. I have shown that, even in the absence of any witness to women's experiences in their own words, a detailed reconstruction of one woman's life can be written based on the available evidence.

My approach improves on previous studies of women's lives in biblical or Iron Age Israel because it does not rely heavily on a single source; instead, multiple sources were consulted to create as complete a picture as possible of women's everyday activities and lifecycle events. Despite the availability of archaeological remains and other sources that inform on women's activities in the Iron Age household, many scholars continue to look solely to the Hebrew Bible when investigating Israelite women. This approach does nothing to correct the incomplete and androcentric perspective of life in ancient Israel that is still presented to the public in popular publications, including many of the recent fictional works on the lives of biblical characters, and scholarly works. My study questions the perception that Israelite women were "submissive chattel in an oppressive patriarchy" (Meyers 1988, back cover), a notion that has been strongly challenged by Carol Meyers and others for more than two decades but is still not widely understood or accepted today.

Additionally, unlike many previous works about biblical women, this book does not focus on what we can know of women's religious lives according to the biblical text. I have illustrated how women's religious experiences should not be separated from their everyday lives; instead, religious belief and practice were probably integrated into daily-life activities, which is seen in the gestures and offerings made in Orah's household a few days after she is born in Chapter 1, and in the rituals that accompanied Orah's funeral and mortuary cult in Chapter 7. Although Orah's birth family and that of her husband participate in the yearly pilgrimage to Yahweh's shrine at Shiloh, the locus of everyday worship is the household. These household rituals are particularly important in the context of lifecycle events such as Orah's first menstruation in Chapter 3, when Astarte is invoked, and the birth of Orah's first child in Chapter 5, when a midwife and female family members perform various acts to protect Orah and her new baby from harmful forces. Women's everyday religious expressions were probably not distinct from their other routine activities, just as religious observance is part of the everyday lives of many people today.

My decision to include a fictional narrative that focuses on one woman's life distinguishes this book from other works on daily life in ancient Israel written by biblical scholars and archaeologists. Focusing on the life of one specific fictional woman allowed me to imagine what life might have been like for a woman at various stages in her life, and led me to investigate the complexity of women's everyday experiences in a rural setting. Although the important men in Orah's life — her father, husband and son — are present in the book, their actions are secondary to the story and the academic discussion that follows; my primary interest was the world of women and their everyday experiences and interactions with each other. Only two other characters in the book are actually named — Orah's older sister Adah, who is the most important figure in Orah's young life, and her daughter Hilah, who was very close to Orah in her final years — in order to highlight female relationships and keep the reader's attention focused on women's activities. I did not originally intend to leave men out of the discussion altogether, but as the events in Orah's life unfolded, the male characters faded into the background. This is quite different from traditional discussions of life in ancient Israel, in which presumed male activities take center stage while women's activities and experiences are often peripheral.

Unlike the recent popular novels about the lives of female biblical characters, the scholarly discussions of the activities and events described in each chapter assure the student and lay reader that the information presented is supported by the archaeological, textual, iconographic and ethnographic sources. The sources for further reading and the other works included in the extensive bibliography are useful to those who want to learn more about the 28 subjects discussed in the book and related topics. Although I assumed that the reader possessed some background in the culture, history and religion of ancient Israel, the discussion is accessible even to those with no prior knowledge. I hope that the fictional account of Orah's life sparked the reader's interest in the subject matter, and will inspire further investigation into the sources that informed this study of women's lives in ancient Israel.

It must be said, however, that the sources consulted in this study are incomplete and subject to varying interpretations. Archaeology supplied much of the information in Chapter 1, which described the background of Orah's family, house and village and provided information about the village economy and the annual agricultural cycle. Chapter 2, which included a discussion of three of the primary "women's activities" in ancient Israel — food preparation, pottery making and textile production — relied heavily on the archaeological material. Throughout the remaining five chapters, archaeological remains from ancient Israel and neighboring areas informed the discussion wherever possible and illustrated the specific household activities in which Orah and the other women in her household would have been engaged. Despite developments in household archaeology and recent interest in identifying gendered spaces in Iron Age households, however, we cannot be absolutely sure that the archaeological remains of presumed female activities were actually used and/or made by women. The same is true of the physical evidence for women's cultic activities in the household context. The best we can do is employ a combination of sources, including texts, iconography and ethnography, to make as strong an argument as possible for the correlation between specific artifacts and installations and women's activities.

The Hebrew Bible was an important source in my reconstruction as well. For certain topics, such as marriage arrangements and wedding customs (Chapter 4) and widowhood (Chapter 7), the biblical text is the primary available source since archaeology and iconography do not inform on these issues. The Hebrew Bible is also an important source for discussing women's roles in public religious life (Chapter 6) and the purity regulations that might have restricted women during menstruation (Chapter 3) and childbirth (Chapter 5). Certain biblical passages with a strong focus on women inspired parts of the narrative; the story of Hannah in 1 Samuel was the inspiration for Chapter 6, which described Orah's family's participation in the pilgrimage to Yahweh's shrine at Shiloh in part to celebrate the weaning of Orah's daughter Hilah. However, as I discussed in the Introduction, using the biblical text to discuss women's experiences is problematic; it must be used cautiously and in tandem with other sources of information. I hope that this book has made quite evident the Bible's limitations as a source for reconstructing the variety of women's daily-life activities and experiences.

Iconographic sources, including the figures in this book, were useful as well, although none of these images was found in an Iron Age I context.

Their relevance for understanding aspects of women's lives in the highland villages is thus unknown, although we can assume some cultural continuity with the artistic representations of females from Iron Age II Judah. Images from neighboring lands, including Phoenicia and Egypt, and from regions a bit more remote, including Cyprus and Assyria, illustrate activities and traditions that we otherwise know relatively little about. The depiction of the female exiles from the city of Lachish on the walls of Sennacherib's palace at Nineveh (Figure 4.2), for example, gives us an indication of the clothing that women and girls in Iron Age Judah might have worn and other hints to their appearance, but, like all of the artistic depictions of women discussed in this book, it was presumably made by a male artist. We are also unsure of how most of the portable objects — such as the pillar figurines (Figure 6.1) — were used, and it is unclear if some of these images depict actual women or goddesses. The archaeological context of the figurines and other representations, when they are known, can inform on the function of the images, but ultimately we do not know how Israelite women would have represented themselves, and if the images that have survived are at all accurate reflections of Iron I women.

The ethnographic sources used in this book derive primarily from nineteenth- and twentieth-century Palestine and Israel with some information from Egypt included as well. In addition, some of the reconstructions in Chapter 1, including those of the four-room house and village layout, are derived from models that are themselves based on ethnographic work carried out in Iran and elsewhere in the Middle East. As noted in the Introduction, ethnographic analogy is unavoidable in archaeological interpretation even when it is not explicitly stated. I have looked to the ethnographic literature from the area under discussion as I believe it most useful for reconstructing activities related to the domestic economy, such as food preparation (Chapter 2) and field activities, including grape harvesting (Chapter 3) and olive picking (Chapter 6). Some of the ethnographic information inspired parts of the story, such as the childbirth practices described in Chapter 5, with the understanding that there is not a one-to-one correspondence between more recent cultural practices and traditions and those of the Iron Age I settlers. The ethnographic documents certainly gave me new insights into aspects of women's labor contributions in traditional village settings.

Despite my efforts to incorporate the various sources of evidence into a holistic reconstruction of one woman's life, not all of the information in the narrative is based on "fact." Although I explain most of the details in the academic discussion that follows in each chapter, parts of the story are fiction and cannot be verified through archaeology or other means. As all who study the ancient world know, reconstructing the past is fraught with difficulties and one must take care when presenting anything about the past as absolutely certain; new discoveries constantly force those of us who work with ancient material to alter our interpretations about things we thought we understood. We can never know everything about the lives of those who came before us, especially those who lived in a place and culture so far removed from our own, but we can use the available sources carefully to create useful models of what life might have been like. These models can then be tested and built upon by future scholars using new evidence as it comes to light, and in doing so more accurate and complete reconstructions of daily life can be written.

I hope that biblical scholars and archaeologists will continue to develop methodologies for researching the lives of women in ancient Israel, as there is still much to learn from the archaeological remains and other underutilized sources about women's activities in ancient Israelite society. Scholars writing about women in ancient Israel would be well advised to direct their scholarship toward a public audience so that unscholarly fictional accounts do not become primary sources of information about women's lives in antiquity. Innovative approaches are needed to both write the lives of Israelite women and disseminate this information to the student and lay reader interested in learning more about the topic but unsure where to locate the most useful and accurate sources. It is my hope that this book is far from the final word on women's lives in biblical times.

Bibliography

Ackerman, S. 1989. "And the Women Knead Dough": The Worship of the Queen of Heaven in Sixth-Century Judah. In *Gender and Difference in Ancient Israel*, ed. P.L. Day, 109–24. Minneapolis: Fortress Press.

——1992. *Under Every Green Tree: Popular Religion in Sixth-Century Judah.* Harvard Semitic Monographs No. 46. Atlanta: Scholars Press.

——2003. Digging up Deborah: Recent Hebrew Bible Scholarship on Gender and the Contribution of Archaeology. *NEA* 66/4: 172–84.

——2008. Asherah, the West Semitic Goddess of Spinning and Weaving? *JNES* 67/1: 1–29.

Albenda, P. 1983. Western Asiatic Women in the Iron Age: Their Image Revealed. *BA* 46/2: 82–88.

Albright, W.F. 1976. Palestinian Inscriptions. A Letter from the Time of Josiah. In *The Ancient Near East*, Vol. II, ed. J.B. Pritchard, 121. Princeton: Princeton University Press.

Amiry, S. and V. Tamari. 1989. *The Palestinian Village Home.* London: British Museum Publications.

Angel, J.L. 1972. Ecology and Population in the Eastern Mediterranean. *WA* 4/1: 88–105.

Avalos, H. 1995. *Illness and Health Care in the Ancient Near East: The Role of the Temple in Greece, Mesopotamia, and Israel.* Atlanta: Scholars Press.

Baadsgaard, A. 2008. A Taste of Women's Sociality: Cooking as Cooperative Labor in Iron Age Syro-Palestine. In *The World of Women in the Ancient and Classical Near East*, ed. B.A. Nakhai, 13–44. Newcastle upon Tyne: Cambridge Scholars.

Bach, A., ed. 1998. *Women in the Hebrew Bible: A Reader.* New York: Routledge.

Barber, E.W. 1994. *Women's Work: The First 20,000 Years. Women, Cloth, and Society in Early Times.* New York: W.W. Norton and Company.

Barkay, G., A.G. Vaughn, M.J. Lundberg and B. Zuckerman. 2004. The Amulets from Ketef Hinnom: A New Edition and Evaluation. *BASOR* 334: 41–71.

Baxter, J.E. 2005. Making Space for Children in Archaeological Interpretations. In *Children in Action: Perspectives on the Archaeology of Childhood*, ed. J.E. Baxter, 77–88. Archaeological Papers of the American Anthropological Association No. 15. Berkeley, CA: University of California Press for the American Anthropological Association.

Bellis, A.O. 1994. *Helpmates, Harlots and Heroes: Women's Stories in the Hebrew Bible*. Louisville: Westminster John Knox Press.

Bird, P. 1997. *Missing Persons and Mistaken Identities: Women and Gender in Ancient Israel*. Minneapolis: Fortress Press.

Blackman, W.S. 1927. *The Fellahin of Upper Egypt*. London: George G. Harrap and Co. Ltd.

Bloch-Smith, E. 1992a. *Judahite Burial Practices and Beliefs about the Dead*. Sheffield: Sheffield Academic Press.

——1992b. The Cult of the Dead in Judah: Interpreting the Material Remains. *JBL* 111/2: 213–24.

——2004. Resurrecting the Iron I Dead. *IEJ* 54/1: 77–91.

Bloch-Smith, E. and B.A. Nakhai. 1999. A Landscape Comes to Life: The Iron I Period. *NEA* 62/2: 62–127.

Bohmbach, K.G. 2000. Companions of Jephthah's Daughter (Judg. 11:37–8). In *WIS*, 244.

Borowski, O. 1998. *Every Living Thing: Daily Use of Animals in Ancient Israel*. Walnut Creek, CA: AltaMira Press.

——2002. *Agriculture in Iron Age Israel*. Boston: American Schools of Oriental Research.

——2003. *Daily Life in Biblical Times*. Atlanta: Society of Biblical Literature.

Braun, J. 2002. *Music in Ancient Israel/Palestine: Archaeological, Written and Comparative Sources*. Grand Rapids, MI: Eerdmans.

Bunimovitz, S. and A. Faust. 2003. Building Identity: The Four-Room House and the Israelite Mind. In *Symbiosis, Symbolism, and the Power of the Past: Canaan, Ancient Israel, and Their Neighbors from the Late Bronze Age through Roman Palaestina*, eds. W.G. Dever and S. Gitin, 411–23. Winona Lake, IN: Eisenbrauns.

Burgh, T. 2006. *Listening to the Artifacts: Music Culture in Ancient Palestine*. New York: T&T Clark International.

Burnette-Bletsch, R. 2000. Lev 15:18–33; 18:19; 20:18: Women and Bodily Emissions. In *WIS*, 205–6.

Burton, A. 2005a. *Abigail's Story* (Women of the Bible). New York: Signet.

——2005b. *Rahab's Story* (Women of the Bible). New York: Signet.

——2006a. *Deborah's Story* (Women of the Bible). New York: Signet.

——2006b. *Jael's Story* (Women of the Bible). New York: Signet.

Byrne, R. 2004. Lie Back and Think of Judah: The Reproductive Politics of Pillar Figurines. *NEA* 67/3: 137–51.

Callaway, J.A. 1984. Village Subsistence at Ai and Raddana in Iron Age I. In *The Answers Lie Below: Essays in Honor of Lawrence Edmund Toombs*, ed. H.O. Thompson, 51–66. Lanham, MD: University Press of America.

Camp, C.V. 1985. *Wisdom and the Feminine in the Book of Proverbs*. Decatur, GA: Almond Press.

Canaan, T. 1933. The Palestinian Arab House: Its Architecture and Folklore. *JPOS* XII: 1–83.

Card, O.S. 2001. *Sarah* (Women of Genesis). New York: Forge Books.

——2002. *Rebekah* (Women of Genesis). New York: Forge Books.

——2005. *Rachel and Leah* (Women of Genesis). New York: Forge Books.

Carter, C.E. 1997. Ethnoarchaeology. In *OEANE* 2, 280–84.

Curtis, R.I. 2001. *Ancient Food Technology*. Leiden: Brill.

Daviau, P.M.M. 2001. Family Religion: Evidence for the Paraphernalia of the Domestic Cult. In *The World of the Aramaeans II: Studies in History and Archaeology in Honour of Paul-Eugene Dion*, eds. P.M.M. Daviau, J.W. Wevers and M. Weigl, 199–229. Sheffield: Sheffield Academic Press.

Dayagi-Mendels, M. 1989. *Perfumes and Cosmetics in the Ancient World*. Jerusalem: The Israel Museum.

——1999. *Drink and Be Merry: Wine and Beer in Ancient Times*. Jerusalem: The Israel Museum.

Dever, W.G. 1993. Gezer. In *NEAEHL* 2, 496–506.

——2002. *What Did the Biblical Writers Know and When Did They Know It?: What Archaeology Can Tell Us About the Reality of Ancient Israel*. Grand Rapids, MI: Eerdmans.

—2003. *Who Were the Early Israelites and Where Did They Come From?* Grand Rapids, MI: Eerdmans.

Ebeling, J.R. 2002. Why Are Ground Stone Tools Found in Middle and Late Bronze Age Burials? *NEA* 65/2: 149–51.

Ebeling, J.R. and M.M. Homan 2008. Baking and Brewing Beer in the Israelite Household: A Study of Women's Cooking Technology. In *The World of Women in the Ancient and Classical Near East*, ed. B.A. Nakhai, 45–62. Newcastle upon Tyne: Cambridge Scholars.

Ebeling, J.R. and Y.M. Rowan. 2004. The Archaeology of the Daily Grind: Ground Stone tools and Food Production in the Southern Levant. *NEA* 67/2: 108–17.

Edghill, I. 2002. *Queenmaker: A Novel of King David's Queen*. New York: St. Martin's Press.

———2004. *Wisdom's Daughter: A Novel of Solomon and Sheba*. New York: St. Martin's Press.

Edwards, D. 1992. Dress and Ornamentation. In *ABD* 2, 232–38.

Epstein, C. 1993. Oil Production in the Golan Heights during the Chalcolithic Period. *Tel Aviv* 20: 133–46.

Etzioni-Halevy, E. 2005. *The Song of Hannah*. New York: Plume.

———2007. *The Garden of Ruth*. New York: Plume.

———2008. *The Triumph of Deborah*. New York: Plume.

Exum, J.C. 1983. "You Shall Let Every Daughter Live": A Study of Exodus 1.8–2.10. *Semeia* 38: 63–82.

———2000. Second Thoughts on Secondary Characters: Women in Exodus 1.8–2.10. In *A Feminist Companion to Exodus-Deuteronomy*, ed. A. Brenner, 75–87. Sheffield: Sheffield Academic Press.

Faust, A. 2004. Mortuary Practices, Society and Ideology: The Lack of Iron Age I Burials in the Highlands in Context. *IEJ* 54, 174–90.

———2006. *Israel's Ethnogenesis: Settlement, Interaction, Expansion and Resistance*. London: Equinox.

Faust, A. and S. Bunimovitz. 2003. The Four Room House: Embodying Iron Age Israelite Society. *NEA* 66/1–2: 22–31.

Finkelstein, I. 1992. Shiloh. In *NEAEHL* 4, 1364–70.

———1993. The History and Archaeology of Shiloh from the Middle Bronze Age II to Iron Age II. In *Shiloh: The Archaeology of a Biblical Site*, eds. I. Finkelstein, S. Bunimovitz and Z. Lederman, 371–93. Tel Aviv: The Institute of Archaeology, Tel Aviv University.

Finkelstein, I., S. Bunimovitz and Z. Lederman, eds. 1993. *Shiloh: The Archaeology of a Biblical Site*. Tel Aviv: Tel Aviv University.

Finley, H. 2001. What Did Women Use for Menstruation in Europe and America from 1700–1900, and Probably Earlier? Museum of Menstruation. http://www.mum.org/whatwore.htm (accessed 5 September, 2007).

Forbes, R.J. 1966. *Studies in Ancient Technology*. Vol. 5. Leiden: Brill.

Frankel, R., S. Avitsur and E. Ayalon. 1994. *History and Technology of Olive Oil in the Holy Land*. Trans. J.C. Jacobson. Tel Aviv: Eretz Israel Museum.

Frick, F.S. 2000. Widows (Exod 22:22, 24; etc.). In *WIS*, 197–99.

Friend, G. 1998. *Tell Taannek, 1963–1968, III/2: The Loom Weights*. Birzeit: Palestinian Institute of Archaeology, Birzeit University.

Frink, L. and K. Weedman. 2005. Introduction to Gender and Hide Production. In *Gender and Hide Production*, eds. L. Frink and K. Weedman, 1–12. Walnut Creek, CA: AltaMira Press.

Frymer-Kensky, T. 2004. *Reading the Women of the Bible: A New Interpretation of Their Stories.* New York: Schocken.

Gonen, R. 1992. The Late Bronze Age. In *The Archaeology of Ancient Israel,* ed. A. Ben-Tor, 211–57. New Haven and London: Yale University Press.

Graham-Brown, S. 1980. *Palestinians and Their Society, 1880–1946.* London and New York: Quartet.

Granqvist, H.N. 1931. *Marriage Conditions in a Palestinian Village.* Vol. 1. Helsingfors: Soderstrom.

——1935. *Marriage Conditions in a Palestinian Village.* Vol. 2. Helsingfors: Soderstrom.

——1947. *Birth and Childhood among the Arabs, Studies in a Mohammadan Village in Palestine.* Helsingfors: Soderstrom.

——1981. *Portrait of a Palestinian Village.* Ed. Karen Seger. London: Third World Centre for Research and Publication.

Grant, E. 1907. *The People of Palestine.* Philadelphia and London: J.B. Lippincott.

Grassi, J.A. 1992. Child, Children. In *ABD* 1, 904–7.

Green, J. 2007. Anklets and the Social Construction of Gender and Age in the Late Bronze and Early Iron Age Southern Levant. In *Archaeology and Women: Ancient and Modern Issues,* eds. S. Hamilton, R.D. Whitehouse and K.I. Wright, 283–311. Walnut Creek, CA: Left Coast Press.

Gruber, M.I. 1992. *The Motherhood of God and Other Studies.* Atlanta: Scholars Press.

——2000a. Puah. In *WIS,* 137–38.

——2000b. Nurse of Joash (2 Kgs 11:2–3; 2 Chr 22:11–12). In *WIS,* 277.

Gursky, M.D. 2001. Reproductive Rituals in Biblical Israel. Unpublished Ph.D. Dissertation, New York University.

Hadley, J. 2000. *The Cult of Asherah in Ancient Israel and Judah: Evidence for a Hebrew Goddess.* Cambridge: Cambridge University Press.

Hallote, R.S. 2001. *Death, Burial, and Afterlife in the Biblical World: How the Israelites and Their Neighbors Treated the Dead.* Chicago: Ivan R. Dee.

Halter, M. 2005. *Sarah* (Canaan Trilogy). New York: Three Rivers Press.

——2006. *Zipporah, Wife of Moses* (Canaan Trilogy). New York: Three Rivers Press.

——2007. *Lilah* (Canaan Trilogy). New York: Three Rivers Press.

Hamilton, V.P. 1992. Marriage: Old Testament and Ancient Near East. In *ABD* 4, 559–69.

Haran, M. 1977. *Temples and Temple-Service in Ancient Israel: An Inquiry into Biblical Cult Phenomena and the Historical Setting of the Priestly School.* Oxford: Clarendon Press.

Herr, L.G. 1997. The Iron Age II Period: Emerging Nations. *BA* 60/3: 114–83.

Hiebert, P.S. 1989. "Whence Shall Help Come to Me?" The Biblical Widow. In *Gender and Difference in Ancient Israel*, ed. P.L. Day, 125–41. Minneapolis: Augsburg Fortress.

Holladay, J.S. 1992. House, Israelite. In *ABD* 3, 308–18.

Homan, M.M. 2002. Beer Production by Throwing Bread into Water: A New Interpretation of Qoh. XI 1–2. *VT* 52/2: 275–78.

——2004. Beer, Barley, and *shekar* in the Hebrew Bible. In *Le-David Maskil: A Birthday Tribute for David Noel Freedman*, eds. R. E. Friedman and W. H. C. Propp, 25–38. Winona Lake, IN.: Eisenbrauns.

Hopkins, D.C. 1987. Life on the Land: The Subsistence Struggles of Early Israel. *BA* 50: 178–91.

Ilan, T. 2003. Dance and Gender in Ancient Jewish Sources. *NEA* 66/3: 135–36.

Irvin, D. 1997. Clothing. In *OEANE* 2, 38–40.

Kamp, K.A. 2001. Where Have All the Children Gone?: The Archaeology of Childhood. *Journal of Archaeological Method and Theory* 8/1: 1–34.

Keel, O. and C. Uehlinger. 1998. *Gods, Goddesses, and Images of God in Ancient Israel*. Minneapolis: Fortress Press.

Killebrew, A. 2005. *Biblical Peoples and Ethnicity: An Archaeological Study of Egyptians, Canaanites, Philistines, and Early Israel, 1300–1100* B.C.E. Atlanta: Society of Biblical Literature.

Kilmer, A.D. 1987. Appendix C: The Brick of Birth. *JNES* 46: 211–13.

King, P.J. and L.E. Stager. 2001. *Life in Biblical Israel*. Louisville: Westminster John Knox Press.

Klein, A. 2007. God Gets a Rewrite: In the Latest Literary Trend, Authors Fictionalize Jewish Heroes. *JewishJournal.com*. http://www.jewishjournal.com (accessed 5 September, 2007).

Kletter, R. 1996. *The Judean Pillar-Figurines and the Archaeology of Asherah*. BAR International Series 636. Oxford: Tempvs Reparatvm.

——2002. People without Burials? The Lack of Iron I Burials in the Central Highlands of Palestine. *IEJ* 52: 28–48.

Lemaire, A. 1992. Education (Israel). In *ABD* 2, 305–12.

Leonard, A., Jr. 1989. The Late Bronze Age. *BA* 52/1: 4–39.

——2003. The Late Bronze Age. In *Near Eastern Archaeology: A Reader*, ed. S. Richard, 349–56. Winona Lake, IN: Eisenbrauns.

Lewis, T.J. 1989. *Cults of the Dead in Ancient Israel and Ugarit*. Ed. F.M. Cross. Harvard Semitic Monographs No. 39. Atlanta: Scholars Press.

Limmer, A. 2007. The Social Functions and Ritual Significance of Jewelry in the Iron Age II Southern Levant. Unpublished Ph.D. Dissertation, University of Arizona.

London, G.A. 2008. Fe(male) Potters as the Personifications of Individuals, Places, and Things as Known from Ethnoarchaeological Studies. In *Women in the Ancient and Classical Near East*, ed. B.A. Nakhai, 155–80. Newcastle upon Tyne: Cambridge Scholars Press.

London, G.A. and M. Sinclair. 1991. An Ethnoarchaeological Survey of Potters in Jordan. In *Madaba Plains Project: The 1987 Season at Tell el-'Umeiri and Vicinity and Subsequent Studies*, eds. L.G. Herr, L.T. Geraty, O.S. LaBianca and R.W. Younker, 420–28. Berrien Springs, MI: Andrews University Press.

MacDonald, N. 2008. *What Did the Ancient Israelites Eat? Diet in Biblical Times*. Grand Rapids, MI: Eerdmans.

Marsman, H.J. 2003. *Women in Ugarit and Israel: Their Social and Religious Position in the Context of the Ancient Near East*. Leiden: Brill.

Matson, F.R. 2001. Potters and Pottery in the Ancient Near East. In *CANE* 3, 1553–65.

Mazar, A. 1992. *Archaeology of the Land of the Bible, Volume 1: 10,000–586 B.C.E.* New Haven: Yale University Press.

——2003. Ritual Dancing in the Iron Age. *NEA* 66/3: 126–32.

McGeough, K. 2006. Birth Bricks, Potter's Wheels, and Exodus 1,16. *Biblica* 87/3: 305–18.

McGovern, P. 2003. *Ancient Wine: The Search for the Origins of Viniculture*. Princeton: Princeton University Press.

Merrillees, R.S. and J. Evans. 1989. Highs and Lows in the Holy Land: Opium in Biblical Times. *Eretz-Israel* 20: 148*–54*.

Meyers, C.L. 1988. *Discovering Eve: Ancient Israelite Women in Context*. Oxford: Oxford University Press.

——1991. "To Her Mother's House" — Considering a Counterpart to the Israelite *Bet 'ab*. In *The Bible and the Politics of Exegesis: Essays in Honor of Norman K. Gottwald on His Sixty-Fifth Birthday*, ed. D. Jobling, P. Day and G. Sheppard, 39–51, 304–7. New York: Pilgrim Press.

——1997. Recovering Objects, Re-visioning Subjects: Archaeology and Feminist Biblical Study. In *A Feminist Companion to Reading the Bible: Approaches, Methods and Strategies*, eds. A. Brenner and C. Fontane, 270–84. London: Firtzroy Dearborn.

——1998. Everyday Life: Women in the Period of the Hebrew Bible. In *Women's Bible Commentary Expanded Edition*, eds. C.A. Newsome and S.H. Ringe, 251–59. Louisville: Westminster John Knox Press.

——1999a. "Women of the Neighborhood" (Ruth 4.17): Informal Female

Networks in Ancient Israel. In *Ruth and Esther: The Feminist Companion to the Bible*, ed. A. Brenner, 110–27. Sheffield: Sheffield Academic Press.

——1999b. Guilds and Gatherings: Women's Groups in Ancient Israel. In *Realia Dei: Essays in Archaeology and Biblical Interpretation in Honor of Edward F. Campbell, Jr. at His Retirement*, eds. P.H. Williams, Jr. and T. Hiebert, 154–84. Atlanta: Scholars Press.

——2000a. Daughters of Israel Lamenting Jephthah's Daughter (Judg. 11:40). In *WIS*, 244–45.

——2000b. Midwife (Gen 35:17; 38:28). In *WIS*, 182–83.

——2000c. Mourning Women (Jer 9:17–20; Ezek 32:16). In *WIS*, 327–28.

——2000d. Female Sorcerer (Exod 22:18; Isa 57:3). In *WIS*, 197.

——2002a. Having Their Space and Eating There Too: Bread Production and Female Power in Ancient Israelite Households. *Nashim: A Journal of Jewish Women's Studies and Gender Issues* 5: 14–44.

——2002b. From Household to House of Yahweh: Women's Religious Culture in Ancient Israel. In *Congress Volume Basel 2001*, ed. A. Lemaire, 277–303. Leiden: Brill.

——2002c. Tribes and Tribulations: Retheorizing Earliest "Israel." In *Tracking "The Tribes of Yahweh": On the Trail of a Classic*, ed. R. Boer, 35–45. London: Continuum.

——2003a. Material Remains and Social Relations: Women's Culture in Agrarian Households of the Iron Age. In *Symbiosis, Symbolism, and the Power of the Past: Canaan, Ancient Israel, and Their Neighbors from the Late Bronze Age through Roman Palaestina*, eds. W.G. Dever and S. Gitin, 425–44. Winona Lake, IN: Eisenbrauns.

——2003b. Engendering Syro-Palestinian Archaeology: Reasons and Resources. *NEA* 66/4: 185–97.

——2005. *Households and Holiness: The Religious Culture of Israelite Women*. Minneapolis: Fortress Press.

——2006. Hierarchy or Heterarchy? Archaeology and the Theorizing of Israelite Society. In *Confronting the Past: Archaeological and Historical Essays on Ancient Israel in Honor of William G. Dever*, eds. S. Gitin, J.E. Wright and J.P. Dessel, 245–54. Winona Lake, IN: Eisenbrauns.

——2007. From Field Crops to Food: Attributing Gender and Meaning to Bread Production in Iron Age Israel. In *The Archaeology of Difference: Gender, Ethnicity, Class and the "Other" in Antiquity. Studies in Honor of Eric M. Meyers*, eds. D.R. Edwards and C.T. McCollough, 67–84. Winona Lake, IN: Eisenbrauns.

Meyers, C.L., T. Craven and R. Kramer, eds. 1998. *Women in Scripture: A Dictionary of Named and Unnamed Women in the Hebrew Bible, the*

Apocryphal/Deuterocanonical Books and the New Testament. Louisville: Westminster John Knox Press.

Murdock, G.P. and C. Provost. 1973. Factors in the Division of Labor by Sex: A Cross-Cultural Analysis. *Ethnology* 12: 203–25.

Nakhai, B.A. 2001. *Archaeology and the Religions of Canaan and Israel*. Boston: American Schools of Oriental Research.

——2005. Daily Life in the Ancient Near East: New Thoughts on an Old Topic. *Religious Studies Review* 31/3–4, 147–53.

——2007. Gender and Archaeology in Israelite Religion. *Religion Compass* 1/5, 512–28.

Neufeld, E. 1971. Hygiene Conditions in Ancient Israel (Iron Age). *BA* 34/2: 41–66.

Newsom, C.A. and S.H. Ringe, eds. 1998. *The Women's Bible Commentary: Expanded Edition with Apocrypha*. Louisville: Westminster John Knox Press.

Nielsen, K. 1992. Incense. In *ABD* 3, 404–9.

Peterson, J. 2002. *Sexual Revolutions: Gender and Labor at the Dawn of Agriculture*. Walnut Creek, CA: AltaMira Press.

Philip, T.S. 2005. *Menstruation and Childbirth in the Bible: Fertility and Impurity*. Studies in Biblical Literature 88. New York: Peter Lang.

Pitard, W.T. 1994. The "Libation Installations" of the Tombs at Ugarit. *BA* 57/1: 20–37.

Platt, E.E. 1992. Jewelry, Ancient Israelite. In *ABD* 3, 823–34.

Pritchard, J.B., 1969. *The Ancient Near East in Pictures Relating to the Old Testament*. 2nd edn. with Supplement. Princeton: Princeton University Press.

Pritchard, J.B., ed. 1976. *The Ancient Near East Volume II: A New Anthology of Texts and Pictures*. Princeton: Princeton University Press.

Robins, G. 1993. *Women in Ancient Egypt*. Cambridge: Harvard University Press.

Rosen, B. 1994. Subsistence Economy in Iron Age I. In *From Nomadism to Monarchy: Archaeological and Historical Aspects of Early Israel*, eds. I. Finkelstein and N. Na'aman, 339–51. Jerusalem: Israel Exploration Society.

Samuel, D. 1999. Bread Making and Social Interactions at the Amarna Workmen's Village, Egypt. *WA* 31/1: 121–44.

Schloen, J.D. 2001. *The House of the Father as Fact and Symbol: Patrimonialism in Ugarit and the Ancient Near East*. Winona Lake, IN: Eisenbrauns.

Sered, S.S. 1992. *Women as Ritual Experts: The Religious Lives of Elderly Jewish Women in Jerusalem*. New York: Oxford University Press.

Sheffer, A. and A. Tidhar. 1991. Textiles and Basketry at Kuntillat 'Ajrud. *'Atiqot* 20: 1–26.

Stager, L.E. 1983. The Finest Olive Oil in Samaria. *Journal of Semitic Studies* 28/1: 241–5.

———1985. The Archaeology of the Family in Ancient Israel. *BASOR* 260: 1–35.

Stol, M. 2000. *Birth in Babylonia and the Bible: Its Mediterranean Setting.* Cuneiform Monographs 14. Groningen: Styx Publications.

Trible, P. 1984. *Texts of Terror: Literary-Feminist Readings of Biblical Narratives.* Minneapolis: Augsburg Fortress Press.

Ussishkin, D. 1982. *The Conquest of Lachish by Sennacherib.* Tel Aviv: The Institute of Archaeology, Tel Aviv University.

Vamosh, M.F. 2008. *Women at the Time of the Bible.* Herzlia, Israel: Palphot.

Vanderkam, J.C. 1992. Calendars: Ancient Israelite and Jewish. In *ABD* 1, 814–20.

van der Toorn, K. 1994. *From Her Cradle to Her Grave: The Role of Religion in the Life of the Israelite and the Babylonian Woman.* Trans. S.J. Denning-Bolle. Sheffield: Sheffield Academic Press.

———2003. Nine Months among the Peasants in the Palestinian Highlands: An Anthropological Perspective on Local Religion in the Early Iron Age. In *Symbiosis, Symbolism, and the Power of the Past: Canaan, Ancient Israel, and Their Neighbors from the Late Bronze Age through Roman Palaestina*, eds. W.G. Dever and S. Gitin, 393–410. Winona Lake, IN: Eisenbrauns.

van Driel-Murray, C. 2000. Leatherwork and Skin Products. In *AEMT*, 299–319.

Vogelsang-Eastwood, G. 2000. Textiles. In *AEMT*, 268–98.

Walsh, C. 2000. *The Fruit of the Vine: Viticulture in Ancient Israel.* Harvard Semitic Monographs 60. Winona Lake, IN: Eisenbrauns.

Wegner, J. 2002. A Decorated Birth-Brick from South Abydos. *Egyptian Archaeology* 20: 3–4.

Wendrich, W.Z. 2000. Basketry. In *AEMT*, 254–67.

Willett, E.A.R. 1999. Women and Household Shrines in Ancient Israel. Unpublished Ph.D. Dissertation, University of Arizona.

———2008. Infant Mortality and Women's Religion in the Biblical Periods. In *The World of Women in the Ancient and Classical Near East*, ed. B.A. Nakhai, 79–98. Newcastle upon Tyne: Cambridge Scholars.

Wilson, C.T. 1906. *Peasant Life in the Holy Land.* London: John Murray.

Younker, R.W. 2003. The Iron Age in the Southern Levant. In *Near*

Eastern Archaeology: A Reader, ed. S. Richard, 367–82. Winona Lake, IN: Eisenbrauns.

Zevit, Z. 2001. *The Religions of Ancient Israel: A Synthesis of Parallactic Approaches*. London: Continuum.

Index

Index

Bes 106–7

bet 'ab 18, 26–8, 31, 81

bet 'em 18, 27–8

Bethel 119

Bethlehem 11, 99, 104

betrothal 85

Bilhah 103

birth (*see* childbirth)

birth brick 102

blood 26–7, 61, 64, 68–70, 96, 103–4, 133

Boaz 134

bone 35, 37, 44, 57, 90, 124, 144

boy 47–8, 90, 96, 98–100, 104, 115, 117, 125

bread 4, 17–18, 32–3, 43–6, 48–51, 53, 55–6, 62, 68, 76–7, 109–10, 122

breastfeeding 19, 116, 118

brewing 4, 18, 44, 48, 51, 53

bride 81, 83–6, 93, 97

bride price 56, 83

burial 21n. 17, 72, 101, 105, 111, 116, 130–1, 133, 139–40, 146n. 3

   cave 106

   customs 146n. 3

   marker 143

cake 44, 46, 49–51, 62, 64, 68, 76–7, 144

calendar 1, 4–6, 37–40, 47

Canaan 12, 14–16, 34, 65, 84, 86, 138

Canaanites 12, 13–17, 21n. 16, 21n. 17, 39, 76, 89, 91, 126, 144

cemetery 20, 131, 140, 145

Central Highlands 1, 5, 9, 12, 14–17, 25–6, 33, 37, 47, 55, 58, 125

ceramics (*see* pottery)

charm 104–5, 107, 144

cherubim 21n. 10, 120

child, children 16, 19, 23–5, 27, 32, 35–6, 40–1, 44–8, 54, 59, 62–3, 66, 71, 76–7, 83, 86, 91–2, 95–8, 100–5, 107–11, 113–19, 121, 124–6, 127n. 3, 129, 131, 134–6, 138, 148

childbirth 2, 4, 9, 11, 45, 78, 90, 95, 98, 100–6, 109, 126, 132, 149–50

circumcised, circumcision 97, 103–4

cistern 30, 34

clay 24, 44, 51, 54–5, 57–8, 62, 66, 71, 73–5, 77, 87, 96–7, 109, 113, 121

cloth, cloths 17, 32, 36, 43–4, 49–50, 56–8, 61–2, 69–70, 73, 91, 96, 103, 107, 130, 144

clothes, clothing 19, 25, 32, 36, 56, 58, 63, 68–9, 71, 80, 86, 90–3, 105, 122–3, 125, 130, 133–4, 137, 141, 150

   belt 63, 91, 122

   cloak 91, 93, 130, 140

   ketonet 91

   ketonet passim 91

   mantle 85, 91, 93

   simla 91

   undergarments 61, 91

concubine 15–16, 23, 27–8, 44, 54–6, 61, 80, 83, 85, 116, 133, 140

cosmetic palette 106

courtyard 24–6, 28, 30, 32–3, 36, 43–4, 50–1, 54–5, 58, 61–2, 70, 80–1, 95, 97, 114, 116, 130

covenant 85, 103, 146n. 4

cult stand 124

Cyprus 14, 54, 60, 77, 138, 150

dance, dancing 19, 64, 80, 87, 89–90, 96, 124

daughter 18–20, 23–5, 40, 45, 48, 56, 60n. 2, 67–8, 73, 75, 81, 84–6, 89, 91, 98, 102, 104, 109, 113, 115–16, 119, 129–31, 134, 136, 141, 145, 148–9

David 16, 82, 84, 87, 89, 91, 106, 122, 138

death 2, 4, 5, 20, 39, 68, 84, 117, 119, 129, 131, 133–7, 139–47

Deborah (Judge) 9, 18, 89, 115, 126

Deborah (Rebekah's nurse) 119

Delilah 84

demon 95, 105

descent, patrilineal 27, 81

Index

diet 18, 33–4, 36–7, 48
Dinah 3, 84
diviner 126
divorce 28, 86, 133, 144
    contract 85
dough 10, 48, 50–1, 62, 76
dowry 83, 93, 134–5

Edom 16
education 5, 18, 47–8, 50, 60n. 2
Egypt 2, 7–12, 14–16, 21n. 16, 26–7, 36, 49,
    51–2, 57–9, 65, 67, 69, 76, 83, 87, 91, 98,
    102, 104–6, 108–9, 117, 119, 122–3, 138,
    141, 150
Egyptian 14–15, 27–8, 36, 58, 65, 68, 74–6,
    84, 87–9, 98, 102, 106, 123
Eli 53
Elisha 138
Elkanah 117, 125
'elohim 143
Enaim 133
Endor 126, 138, 140, 143
Ephrath/Bethlehem 99
Er 134
Esau 94n. 1
evil
    eye 105–7
    spirit 101, 106, 138

father 15–16, 21, 23–4, 27–8, 43–5, 48,
    54–5, 60n. 2, 62, 67, 69, 73, 75–6, 79–86,
    89, 101, 103, 131–5, 140, 147–8
feast 26, 37, 40, 43–5, 82, 85, 93, 97,
    113–15, 120, 124–5, 127, 130–1
fertility 19, 25, 68–9, 76–7, 80, 83, 86, 98,
    101–2, 113, 117, 119, 126, 131–2, 137–9,
    143–2
fibulae 90, 140
fig 34, 110
figurine
    pillar 10, 116, 118, 127n. 2, 150
    plaque 87
flax 57

four-room house 18, 29, 30–2, 70, 102,
    150
fruit 19, 34, 36, 38–9, 40, 46, 51–2, 55, 57,
    72, 79–80, 83, 95, 110, 120
funeral 71, 141, 148
funerary ritual 20, 139–41

Gaza Strip 138
Gezer 17, 38, 84
Gezer Calendar 5, 38–9, 47
Gideon 47
gift 45, 64, 78, 80–1, 83–5, 124, 127, 131,
    135
girl 2, 5, 16, 18, 23–4, 35, 37, 40, 45–8, 56,
    59, 60n. 2, 63–4, 67–8, 74–5, 84, 91, 100,
    103–4, 114–17, 124, 141, 150
goats' hair 49, 56–7
god 2, 8, 23–4, 26, 40, 44–5, 69, 73, 75–6,
    81, 95–7, 100, 106, 126, 132, 143, 145,
    146n. 4
goddess 10, 19, 25, 30, 44, 56, 62–4, 74,
    76–8, 87, 102, 118, 126, 131, 143, 146n. 4,
    150
gold 74, 80, 83, 85, 89, 93, 124
Gomer 117
grain 5, 24–5, 30, 33–6, 38–40, 43–5,
    49–52, 55, 62, 89–90, 109, 114, 120, 123,
    129, 131, 137
grandmother 23, 25, 27, 54, 129, 136
grape 19, 33–4, 61–7, 89, 109–10
    harvest 39, 45, 61, 64–6, 78, 150
grinding 33, 44, 48–51, 59, 89, 137
grinding stones, ground stone tools 24, 43,
    48–50, 58, 129
    grinding slab 34, 49–50
    handmill 50
    handstone 49–50, 131, 140
    mortar 49, 73, 113, 121–2
    pestle 113, 121–2
    quern 49–50

Hagar 83, 122
hag haqqasir 40

Index

Index

Index

Index